The Pe

The story of Peter Wing
North America's First Chinese Mayor

By T.D. Roth

Tellwell Talent
www.tellwell.ca

ISBN
978-1-77302-411-0 (Paperback)
978-1-77302-412-7 (eBook)

Inside cover art: The Chinese characters are Eng Wing Him's name.

Table of Contents

Lin, Peter, Kim and Eng Wing at Peter's Mayoral Inauguration, January 1966
(Photo Kamloops Museum & Archives #6877)

Author's Note

This is the story of Peter Wing, the first Chinese mayor in North America. It is set in the larger context of the thousands of Chinese coming to Canada in the 19th and early 20th centuries. Some came seeking temporary employment and riches from the *Gold Mountain.* Others sought a new life and a new identity in a culture that denied their recognition as human beings and withheld their participation in the political process. In many ways it is the story of Peter Wing's father, Eng Wing, who guided his family through World War I, the Spanish Flu, the Great Depression and World War II; who taught his children to deal with the racial prejudice of a predominantly British society; and who quietly intertwined his family into the fabric of the local community of Kamloops, British Columbia.

What was it that made Peter Wing such a remarkable person? He led no demonstrations or great movements. He accomplished no great feats. Yet, he was a truly exceptional person. And what was it about Kamloops, British Columbia that a first-generation Chinese Canadian could become mayor? Why not a large city such as San Francisco or Seattle or Vancouver where there are sizable Chinese communities? Is there something new immigrants can learn from Peter Wing's family?

Is there something second and third-generation Canadians can learn from Peter? Can his life story help you and me be better Canadians?

When I first set out to write Peter Wing's story I had been living in Canada for over twenty years as a landed immigrant. As a Caucasian coming from the United States my experience hardly compares to the struggles and fears of the early Chinese immigrants. Yet, my wife and I once experienced temporary detention when returning to Canada from the United States and were told by an official, "I can keep you here as long as it takes to check your documents." It was a frightening experience. Our little children were with friends in St. John's, Newfoundland and we had no immediate way of contacting them. During those years we took no part in elections and always felt a bit insecure, knowing that we did not have the full rights and security offered by Canadian citizenship. What resonates about Peter's story is the journey that all immigrants take in assuming a new national identity. We owe a great debt to the Canadian Chinese and other early immigrants that came before us. After many hours with Mr. Wing and his wife, Kim, I am honoured to share their story. Where possible, you will read their own words taken from many hours of personal interviews. My own contribution will be to set their family story into the much larger story of Chinese immigrants and their struggle for recognition as "people" and citizens of the wonderful country we call Canada.

Prologue

Peter Wing's life represents the finest of human values – a supportive team spirit, hard work, patience and integrity. To understand the man, we must glimpse into the history of his people and the culture in which he lived.

Within Peter's genes lay 5,000 years of history and tradition. His Chinese-Canadian heritage represents the experience of a small minority of the thousands of Chinese that came to Canada in the 1800s. The first mention of these immigrants in British North America appeared in *The Victoria Gazette*, June 30th, 1858 under the title, "A Pioneer Chinaman." The term, "pioneer," actually applied to only a very small group of Chinese immigrants, those who came to Canada intending to stay. Among that group was Peter Wing's father.

In the second half of the 19th century the one economic necessity lacking in the Dominion of Canada and in the Province of British Columbia, in particular, was the human resource. Industry needed manpower – reliable, plentiful, cheap labour. In the 1850s a large influx of Chinese men had flooded into the gold fields of British Columbia. They quickly became indispensable labourers not only in the mines, but in the fisheries as well.

In the 1880s the Canadian Pacific Railway saw the Chinese potential for abundant, cheap labour and signed an initial agreement with Chinese contractors to bring 5,000 workers from China. Within a year only 1,500 were still working the rails. Illness and industrial accidents had taken the lives of many, but the majority deserted to work in the gold fields. Gold, though offering no guarantees, could bring a man wealth beyond his imagination. On rail construction crews the white, black and aboriginal labourers earned three dollars a day. Chinese labourers were paid a dollar a day for the same work, though even that seemed a fortune compared to the seven cents a day being paid for labour in China. The Canadian Pacific Railway (CPR) also contracted thousands of Chinese men from California where they had failed to make their fortunes in the gold rush of the 1850s. Sir John A. McDonald, Canada's first Prime Minister, in addressing Parliament in 1882, insisted that rail construction required cheap labour, "It is simply a question of alternatives: either you must have this labour or you can't have the railway." The Chinese were willing to take the undesirable jobs for a pittance. They were hard workers, dependable labourers and willing to take risks. If injured or lost they were easily replaced. Their contribution to the Canadian dream has received little attention. How the west was won may be far different from what is commonly believed.

Yet, as much as the Chinese were needed, they came to a land where their colour, traditions and religion were feared and misunderstood. The Province of British Columbia fought vehemently with the Dominion of Canada for enactment of laws that would restrict, restrain and even prohibit the flow of Chinese into the province. The provincial view was that Chinese labour, though essential to the development of the Province, must be considered as only temporary.

Provincial leaders feared the potential impact of foreigners in a parliamentary democracy. What if these few who came to work were only the vanguard of hordes to come? Provincial legislation passed in 1875 denied voting rights at the provincial level to anyone of Chinese origin. This was followed twenty years later in 1896 with laws that stripped Chinese of voting rights in all municipal elections, effectively removing all political privileges and rights from the Chinese in British Columbia. We can only conjecture, but perhaps there was fear that Chinese representation in government at any level would gradually open the door for massive immigration and a change in the ethnic demographics and cultural traditions of the country. Legislation also barred Chinese from the legal and pharmaceutical professions and employment by provincial and municipal governments. The legislation insured that: Chinese lawyers would never challenge those laws limiting the rights and freedoms of Chinese immigrants; Chinese health professionals would never threaten the established medical community; and Chinese residents would have no influence in provincial or municipal decisions.

Keeping the Chinese in the position of "hewers of wood and bearers of water" would keep them from becoming indispensable to their communities and limit their influence in the development of the country. A prevailing idea of the time was that through expansion of power and influence "Orientals" were a danger to Western civilisation. The phrase "Yellow Peril," first used by the German Emperor Wilhelm II in 1895 when he dreamed that Buddha came riding a dragon against the peoples of Europe, epitomized the emotional fears of white society. This one man's dream quickly became a nightmare for people of Asian descent.

In 1899, in an effort to reduce the Chinese population in British Columbia, "An Act to Regulate Immigration to British Columbia" was passed by the Province. To avoid conflict with the Federal Government of Canada the Chinese were not specifically named. The intent, however, was obvious. The act required that immigrants be able to write a European language. The law took effect January 1st, 1901 and was quickly disallowed by the Dominion of Canada, which needed labourers to finish operational improvements on the CPR, including the Spiral Tunnels through the Kicking Horse Pass and the eight kilometre (five miles) Connaught Tunnel through Mount McDonald.

Fear of the Chinese continued, though the "peril" was for the most part imaginary. It can be argued that if the Chinese were given unregulated immigration and a voice in government, the prevailing British culture would have been threatened. Democracy does not necessarily support a ruling minority. However, the vast majority of Chinese who came to Canada came to make their fortune and then return to China. Peter Wing gave this evaluation of the situation:

"Our people came over to better our lot in one way or another and we were given limited opportunity. That's why there were so few that stayed. They felt that because of discrimination they weren't going to get ahead. Why be a barber or a laundryman or a gardener when you could do the same thing at home and exist in your own area? The United States and Canada, what they called 'The Gold Mountain', didn't accept them as people anyway."

Only a few came with the same mind-set as the European settlers that we look upon as pioneers and today call Canadians. This story revolves around two families that came to stay, the Wings of Kamloops and the Kwongs of Revelstoke, British Columbia.

Chapter 1

THE GOLD MOUNTAIN

*Peace-loving and strong, the ox labours
patiently to bring forth produce from
the ground. (Chinese Proverb)*

For a landless illiterate peasant, working as a steward in an opium den
may have been a source of survival, but it was not a life and offered
no future. As Wing Him Eng closed its door for the last time, he also
closed the door to an unhappy chapter of his life. No more would he
suffer the condescension of the wealthy as they lounged on brocaded
divans in their drug-induced reveries; or witness the haggard bodies
and bloodshot eyes of the addicted; or note the foolishness of men
who, in spite of the hallucinations, the nausea and the headaches,
would come again and again until their family fortunes were gone. The
fate of the elderly placed in a corner with their coveted opium pipe
to end their days in mindless oblivion was not to be his fate. Eng's
uncle, whose name has long been forgotten, had sent him passage to

Kamloops, British Columbia in the land of the *Gold Mountain*. It must have seemed like manna from heaven.

"Father was a servant in an opium den. He had no other abilities," said Peter. *"In Taishan, you were within walking distance of home. You didn't marry within your own village. You took a wife from a neighbouring village and that's it. Father looked forward enough to realize that wasn't what he wanted either for himself or for us."*

In the summer of 1901, the Year of the Ox, Wing Him Eng, age 16, set sail for Canada. He came seeking a new life and carrying a vision different from most who sailed with him: he was a Christian; he had no intention of returning to China; and he was determined to establish a new and better life.

For most Chinese immigrants, Canada was "Gum San," the *Gold Mountain*. A few years in the mines or on the railroad was like harvesting a money tree. In a single week, a man could earn the equivalent of a peasant's yearly wage in his homeland. In only a few years, he could return to China and a life of relative wealth and leisure. The majority of immigrants had neither desire nor intent of settling.

The Chinese extended family, with its traditions and religion, stood as a great obstacle to any permanent emigration outside of China. Their traditional religions, Buddhism and Taoism, upheld a strong commitment to ancestor worship. At the death of the father, the eldest son was responsible to commemorate his father's virtues. Depending on the family status, paper money and paper representations of everyday life, including clothes, servants and even horses, were supplied by the son for his father's journey to the other world. The son was to mourn publicly for three years by wearing white clothing and abstaining from meat, wine and public gatherings.

Tradition also required that families maintain the places of burial and honour their ancestors annually during the Qingming Festival. This "Pure Brightness" festival, also known as "Ancestor's Day," is celebrated annually in the month of April. The festival involves the ritual "sweep of the tombs" (cleaning of the gravesites) and offering of food, tea, wine and libations to the deceased. Such practices would have seemed bizarre and anti-Christian in a Protestant 19th century British society. Christian missionaries, who taught that one must disown father and mother if necessary, found ancestor worship the greatest obstacle to making Asian converts. Traditions such as this placed a cultural chasm between the Chinese and British societies. The young Wing, who had accepted the Christian teaching, would find himself trapped between two seemingly immovable barriers: the religious prejudice of his homeland and the racial prejudice of his new land.

The Chinese cemetery in Kamloops, British Columbia, the oldest known Chinese cemetery in Canada, stands as a witness to the bias of early 20th century British society toward Asian peoples. A rancher named George Bower set aside the site in 1860 for his Chinese ranch hands because the city would not accept Chinese remains in the public cemetery. Much of the Chinese cemetery today is empty, because for many years the site served as a temporary holding ground. When circumstances allowed, the bodies, or more often the bones, were exhumed and returned to China. The Chinese saw this as "falling leaves returning to their roots." This idiom pictured the cycle of life in which the plant gives life to the leaves, which in turn, give life to the plant.

In Buddhist and Taoist tradition, the souls of deceased people will one day be reincarnated, but until that time their souls wander in the area where their bodies are buried. It was very important to Asian families that their husbands and fathers be buried in their homeland and their spirits be near their families.

The Kamloops site became a permanent resting place following World War I when the exhumation and transport of bones was legally banned. In 1956, local Chinese families bought the site, the only remaining landmark of what was once a thriving community, which had included miners, rail workers, merchants, cooks, launderers, cowboys, house servants and labourers. The Kamloops Chinese Cultural Association took responsibility for the cemetery in 1980.

In 1995, out of respect for the deceased who had never returned to their homeland, the Province of Guangdong, China donated two large stone lions to sit at the entrance of the cemetery. The following year the Chinese Consulate to Canada visited the site and ceremonially dotted the lions' eyes, symbolically insuring that they never sleep in their vigil over the departed souls that remain.

Not only did Eng face a clash of religion and culture, the Chinese were a visible minority that wore their own clothing and generally stayed in the "Chinatowns" of their respective communities. The traditional queue or pigtail symbolized their continued allegiance to the Qing dynasty of China. They had no need to learn the language or the customs required to be incorporated into the larger community. Most came to work and had every intention of one day, like their fathers before them, being buried where they were born, in China.

This readily concurred with the government policies of British Columbia, which tightly controlled entry for Asian workers. At the turn of the 20th century, visa restrictions for the province held the male-female ratio of Chinese at about 25 to 1. A $100 head tax, a fixed fee for every Chinese person entering Canada, was levied in 1900 and raised to $500 in 1903. This insured that few wives and children ever reached Canada. The majority of the Chinese already in the province had migrated north from the minefields of California. They were not only good, reliable labour for the railroads, mines and fisheries; they were also good farmers and eventually would own the majority of the land in the Fraser and Thompson River Canyons of British Columbia. Till then these men were considered "guest workers," not settlers.

Laws were also enacted limiting the number of Asian immigrants that ships were allowed to bring to Canada on any given passage: one person per fifty tons of total tonnage rating. At the time, three sister vessels, the RMS Empress of China, the RMS Empress of India and the RMS Empress of Japan regularly sailed between the Orient and British Columbia for the Canadian Pacific Steamship Company. These ships, roughly half the size of the British Columbia coastal ferries, were fitted to carry 50 first class passengers, 150 second-class passengers and, depending on the amount of cargo, 200 to 400 passengers in steerage. With a tonnage rating of 5905, the maximum number of Asians would never have exceeded more than 118 per sailing. With the attrition of immigrant workers through accidents and return to the homeland, the probable goal was a net zero increase in resident Chinese immigrants.

A plaque citing the official apology of the Province of British Columbia to its Chinese people displayed in the Kamloops Chinese Cemetery summarizes the appalling prejudice Eng Wing would face over the next forty-five years when he stepped off the ship at Victoria, British Columbia:

"BE IT RESOLVED that this legislature apologizes for more than a hundred laws, regulations and policies that were imposed by past provincial governments that discriminated against people of Chinese descent since 1871, when British Columbia joined confederation, to 1947. These laws and policies denied British Columbia's Chinese communities' basic human rights, including but not limited to, the right to vote, hold public office, or own property; imposed labour, educational and employment restrictions; subjected them to health and housing segregation, and prevented them from fully participating in society. The House deeply regrets that these Canadians were discriminated against simply because they were of Chinese descent. All members of the House acknowledge that we all aspire to be a fair and just society where people of all nations and cultures are welcomed, accepted and respected.

BE IT FURTHER RESOLVED that the House acknowledges that the Chinese Canadian Community endured untold hardship and persevered with grace and dignity. We acknowledge that despite being subjected to discriminatory laws, policies and practises, the Chinese community has made, and continues to make substantial contributions to the culture, history and economic prosperity in our province."

Wing's voyage, most likely on the *RMS Empress of China,* was not a cruise he spoke of in later years. Departure and arrival dates and times were somewhat random. In 1907, the Canadian Minister of Agriculture reported that the *Empress* had been held in quarantine when a passenger traveling from Hong Kong to Yokohama showed signs of small pox. Passengers and crew alike were detained until the incubation period passed. Similar delays were common.

Upwards of thirty days on the Pacific Ocean in steerage was more of a trial than an adventure. Stale cooking smells, body odours and the unmistakeable reek of vomit ever-present in confined ocean vessels is aptly described by Alfred Steiglitz, an American photographer, in his graphic description of steerage on the luxury liner *Kaiser Wilhelm II*, which sailed the North Atlantic during the same time period.

"...the 900 steerage passengers crowded into the hold...are positively packed like cattle, making a walk on deck when the weather is good, absolutely impossible, while to breathe clean air below in rough weather, when the hatches are down is an equal impossibility. The stenches become unbearable, and many of the emigrants have to be driven down; for they prefer the bitterness and danger of the storm to the pestilential air below.*

"The food, which is miserable, is dealt out of huge kettles into the dinner pails provided by the steamship company. When it is distributed, the stronger push and crowd, so that meals are anything but orderly procedures... in the steerage from 200 to 400 sleep in one compartment on bunks, one above the other, with little light and no comforts." (On the Trail of the Immigrant by Edward A. Steiner, Fleming H. Revell Co., N.Y., 1907)

Stepping onto the dock at Victoria, a thriving city on Vancouver Island located off the west coast of Canada, must have provided a mixed feeling of relief, fear and wonder for Wing and his fellow travellers. Victoria, an enclave of British culture, was alive with movement and opportunity. Some immigrants met their contractors and continued up the coast to the fisheries and logging camps. Others caught the ferries to Vancouver and then traveled north to the mines and the railroads. A few opted to set up shop in the Chinatowns springing up in the larger communities. The money trees of the *Gold Mountain* seemed ripe for the picking. In reality, the first picking was nearly past and only the gleaning remained. Still, Canada represented an opportunity lacking in China.

Wing's first step was registry with Canadian immigration officials. In China the family name came first and given names followed. Wing's full name in China would have been, "Eng Wing Him." Immigration officials read the Chinese names through British eyes and changed the surname to "Wing" and the given name to "Eng" on the government documents.

Wing, from this point, would be known as Eng to his family and associates. With his new name and new beginning, he cut off the pigtail. In China it signified deference to the Chinese emperors, but for Eng their authority stopped at the dock in Victoria. His loyalty would be to his new country. His family, when it came, would be Canadian first and Chinese second.

Eng spoke no English, but with nearly 75 percent of all Chinese in North America coming from the same general area of Taishan in the Guangdong province of China, it was not hard to get directions from other Asian immigrants as he made his way, first by ferry to Vancouver, and then by train to his future home, Kamloops, British Columbia.

His first sight of coastal British Columbia compared favourably to Taishan; rugged peaks, lush vegetation and abundant rainfall. The temperature was a different matter. Tropical Taishan's average temperature of 22.6 degrees Celsius (72.6F) is twice that of temperate Vancouver, which averages 11 degrees Celsius (51.8F). This must have been refreshing to Eng when he first arrived, but as the train gained elevation travelling up the Fraser River Canyon, through the tunnels and into the high country, the sun gained intensity. Eng would soon experience scorching summer temperatures as high as 40 degrees Celsius (104F) and frigid winter temperatures as low as a -25 degrees Celsius (-13F). What a surprise to find himself moving to the northwestern tip of the Great American Desert.

Kamloops must have seemed somewhat bleak. The community is surrounded by sagebrush and sunburnt bunch grass. On the north side of Kamloops Lake, it is not uncommon to encounter rattlesnakes – perhaps explaining why most residents live on the south side. Walking through the hills hikers regularly come upon a miniature prickly pear cactus whose spines are excruciatingly painful when caught in the side of a canvas shoe. Yet within an hour's drive a person can be surrounded by the endless forests and cool mountain lakes of the British Columbia interior. Eng would wait many years before having a car with which to escape the scorching heat of summer. The weather was part of the adventure when he arrived in 1901. His future bride, Lin, would find it more of a trial when she joined him in 1913.

Kamloops was the right place for Eng Wing to begin his new life. The name "Kamloops" comes from the native word "Cumeloups." It was given to the location by Alexander Ross, a trader with the Pacific Fur Company, who visited the site May 16, 1812. It means "the meeting of the waters" and was the original native Secwepemc (Shuswap) word for their camp where the North and South Thompson Rivers come together. The rivers offered natural access into the interior of British Columbia and were well situated for the fur trade with First Nations people. Ross built a trading post on the site in 1812. The Pacific Fur Company was soon bought out by the North West Company, which in turn merged with the Hudson's Bay Company. Four successive forts were built in and around the site. The last, Fort Kamloops, was abandoned in 1872. The building remained intact into the 1940s.

Each spring the muddy waters of the North Thompson River flow and mix with the clear waters of the South Thompson. The result is a larger, stronger river that quickly flows into Kamloops Lake. In a similar manner the different peoples of Kamloops (First Nations, British and American, Italian and German, Chinese and Japanese, Sikh and East Indian) make for a larger, stronger community serving the interior of British Columbia.

The clay cliffs to the southwest of Kamloops made the area very difficult to enter for general settlement and expansion until the completion of the Canadian Pacific Railroad in 1886. Before that, supplies first came by pack animals and later by rail to the small community of Savona located on Kamloops Lake 29 km (17 ½ miles) southwest of Kamloops. Goods and materials were then transferred to sternwheelers, which cruised first to Kamloops and then up the North and South Thompson Rivers. The rivers and larger lakes were the original transportation system. Freight canoes, then sailing vessels, and finally steam ships carried the men, equipment and supplies needed by the early miners, loggers, rail crews and settlers. Kamloops was becoming an important doorway to the provincial interior. The Canadian Pacific and Canadian Northern Railways, when completed, crossed in Kamloops, making the city a vital doorway to Interior British Columbia. Because of its unique location the community was for a brief time considered as a possible candidate for the provincial capital.

In 1901, Kamloops hardly appeared like a place to make one's fortune. More of a village than a city or town, the community was only eight years old and supported a population of about 1,000 people. Like many developing western communities only four streets were paved: Victoria Street, 4th Avenue, 3rd Avenue and Seymour Street. The town ended at 6th Avenue where the main wagon trail, known as the "Corkscrew," wound its way east behind the present Royal Inland Hospital. Since the Canadian Pacific Railway ran down the middle of Victoria Street, locals claimed to have "the longest main street in the world," running from Vancouver to Halifax. Chugging down the main thoroughfare, the train conveniently slowed in passing the clubs at either end of town where patrons could jump off to sample the spirits and ladies of the west.

Eng stepped off the train onto the platform where his uncle had been watching the arrivals for days, possibly even for several weeks. He was expecting a young man in traditional Chinese dress with traditional Chinese grooming and at first glance may have mistaken Eng as one of the local natives. After giving the boy a brief greeting and a good thrashing for cutting off his queue, he introduced Eng to members of the Methodist Chinese Mission. Nothing more is known of this uncle, but Canada owes him a great debt for the remarkable family yet to be born.

The Methodist Chinese Mission, established in 1890, was a godsend to Chinese immigrants hoping to make Canada their permanent home, but the missionaries viewed their work with both religious and cultural objectives. The prevailing goals of 19th and early 20th century missions were: first, the commitment to win souls for Christ, "Therefore go and make disciples of all nations..." (Matthew 28:19, NIV); second, a genuine concern for the social conditions and challenges of immigrant minorities, "Come, you who are blessed by my Father...For I was hungry and you gave me something to eat, I was thirsty and you gave me something to drink, *I was a stranger and you invited me in...*" (Matthew 25:34-35, NIV); and third, and perhaps most controversial, the desire to assimilate Asians into a white Anglo-Saxon culture.

Missionary leaders believed that Orientals must not only be "Christianized," but they must also be "Canadianized." Assimilation was considered vital to remove the perceived perils of Asian vice and paganism: primarily gambling, smoking of opium, female slavery and ancestor worship.

The Wing family would eventually become a model of the mission objective. At the mission, Eng received the basic education denied him in China including literacy in his own native language, Cantonese. At the mission, he learned to speak the rudimentary English so vital in his later business dealings. Through the mission, Eng was placed as house-boy and gardener with the Beattie family of Kamloops. The Beatties, proprietors of the Select School, a private institution run in their home, helped immensely with Eng's grasp of English and his integration into the Canadian culture.

Once Eng could function in English he left the Beatties for work in the CPR Restaurant. Work in the restaurant was more of an appren-ticeship than a goal. Those who mistook Eng's lack of language and education for a lack of intelligence were sorely mistaken. He was a natural born entrepreneur entering the university of life by seizing those opportunities denied him in China.

For Chinese wanting to establish themselves in the community, the traditional Chinese restaurants and laundries required only rudimen-tary English and little technical education. The investment required to open such establishments was also within the reach of the frugal immi-grant. After a short time in the CPR Restaurant Eng saved sufficient money to enter partnerships in not just one, but in two small cafes, The American Cafe (later renamed The Silver Grill on the 200 block of Victoria Street in downtown Kamloops) and The Good Eats (then located on the 300 block of Victoria Street). He still had not achieved his goal. These two restaurants might be viewed as a secondary education leading to more important things. With patience, Eng was positioning himself to attain the sufficient savings and status required for marriage.

Chinese tradition, Methodist belief and British culture made finding a wife in Canada highly unlikely, if not impossible. To seek a Caucasian wife would have been scandalous and unacceptable. Eng's cultural values ran deep within his psyche. Marriage must honour the family. It was far too important to be left to romantic notions and youthful lust. Chinese tradition demanded that marriage be based on family integrity and family ties, not on the elusive emotion Canadians call "love." His clan had lived in a small village in Taishan for generations. Eng would travel to China where his family may have arranged a wife for him while he was still a boy. If there were no family arrangements, then Methodist missionaries would help him find a suitable wife to bring to Canada. *That meant working and waiting for another nine long years.*

Leung Lin, the yet to be chosen bride, would become a source of comfort, children and partnership in giving Canada some of its finest citizens. It is difficult to grasp the single mindedness of a 16-year-old boy working for a pittance, living in self-imposed poverty and saving enough money to pay the return passage for himself and his new wife. By the time Lin entered Canada, the head tax had been raised to $500, the equivalent of two years' wages, a small fortune for any labouring man. Times, of course, were different. Boys went to work at age 13 and quickly became men. Teenage marriage was the norm. A high school education, which few attained, was the equivalent of a secondary degree.

Unfortunately, Eng revealed very little of his past to his children and Lin revealed even less of hers. The family stories of their clans were never told. How they met and the details of their marriage were never discussed. Since Eng and Lin were both Christians, we may assume the marriage was under the auspices of the Chinese missionaries and that some of the Chinese traditions, such as the purchase price of the bride, may not have been followed.

"We never had too much discussion except for business or practical purposes," said Peter. *"He was so busy making a living and I was so busy trying to translate from English to Chinese as I grew up, 90 percent of our conversation was to do with business and the aspect of being able to exist in Canada."*

The wedding took place in 1911 in Hoy Ping, Eng's home village. Hoy Ping, spelled "Ho Ping" on maps in the early 1900s, is located on older maps in the province of Kwang-tung. The regional capital was Canton. The specific dialect of Chinese spoken by the family was Taishan, probably a mountain dialect of Cantonese. This dialect is now virtually extinct. The couple could have stayed, but the region offered no future for Eng. The move to Canada had changed him. His peasant dream of "tiles over one's head and soil under one's feet," a portrayal of belonging and permanence, would be realized in Canada. Re-entry into Canada, however, would require another two years of bureaucratic hurdles. British Columbia did not want Asian families taking root in North America.

Eng brought his bride to a social climate that would challenge the Chinese in Canada for many years. In 1911, Louis C. Taylor, a member of the Asiatic Exclusion League, was mayor of Vancouver. The same year, British author, Sax Rohmer, published the first of his Fu Manchu novels. Fu Manchu, a western caricature of the Manchu Dynasty, made interesting reading, but the image of an evil Chinese master criminal only added to prevailing notions of the Yellow Peril and did little to further the fortunes of the Chinese living in the British Empire.

Even at this early time, the Chinese culture within Canada was shifting. The rebellion against the Manchu Dynasty began in 1911, establishing the Republic of China in 1912. That year the Chinese Free Masons of North America passed a resolution calling for their men to cut off their queues, the traditional pigtails expressing loyalty to the emperors. They transferred their support to Sun Yat Sen, founding father of the Republic of China. Sun Yat Sen's "Three Principles of the People" stressing nationalism, democracy and capitalism resonated with those Chinese experiencing western ways. At the same time, North American Chinese were moving away from traditional dress and customs which had isolated them from the west. It seems this shift was not one of integration, but rather, an ideological identification with the revolution in China. These benefitted immigrants like Eng, but there was a difference. The Chinese Free Masons maintained their ties and interests in China. Eng, as an individual, had made similar changes in dress and manner ten years earlier. His ties and interests were in Canada.

Peter knew very little about his mother, Leung Lin. She had no brothers or sisters and no family ties. She was of frail health and suffered chronic, sometimes debilitating, asthma. The climate in Kamloops must have seemed brutal: no central heating in winter; no air conditioning in summer; and no vehicle to escape to the surrounding forests and lakes. She arrived in Kamloops in 1913 as a teenager who spoke no English and had no friends. We can only imagine the sense of isolation and loneliness she must have experienced.

While Eng was in China for his marriage to Lin, a new Mission Superintendent for British Columbia was taking up residence in Kamloops. Dr. Smith Stanley Osterhout had worked with various First Nations peoples in northern British Columbia from 1893 to 1903. In 1911, after two years of language training in China, he took charge of the home missions in British Columbia. Dr. Osterhout's personal involvement and interest in the young Wings would be invaluable to their success and the future of their children.

"For a little while they lived in the Mission," said Peter. *"Then they lived in a room above the restaurant. Dad … was a very practical man. [Mother] was lucky in a way in that there was a Chinese family in Kamloops that had a daughter about the same age as mother that was able to speak enough Chinese to communicate."*

Lin's only security was found in Eng. Together they would exercise the time and patience required to build a family, home and business.

Of necessity, Eng chose to be close to his work; by design, his children would not be exposed to the work crews, the traditions or the

ancestor worship of Chinatown. A community predominately popu-
lated by single working men was not a healthy atmosphere for raising a
family. For many single Chinese men, the chief form of entertainment
was mah-jong, a game similar to rummy that involved a combination
of both skill and chance, a game in which wages earned in hours could
be lost in minutes. And for those who desired it, there was opium.
Even today, the odd opium poppy can be found in the Kamloops area.
The Wing children might be raised in a society that denied them the
legal status of being "people" for another 34 years, but Eng intended
that they always think of themselves as Canadians.

Great challenges lay ahead for those who had come to the *Gold
Mountain* wishing to remain. The silent movies of the 1920s would
bring back the evil Fu Manchu and fuel the stereotypical ideas about
the "Yellow Peril." Chinese immigrants who maintained their homeland traditions would be seen as a threat to Western culture. Chinese
labourers willing to work for low wages would be seen as a threat to
the working class, a highly imaginary danger considering restrictions
imposed on Asian immigration. In 1922, British Columbia would pass
a resolution favouring complete exclusion of all Asians. The following
year, the Dominion of Canada, partially to appease British Columbia,
would pass the Chinese Immigration Act, also known as the Chinese
Exclusion Act, which limited Chinese immigration to consuls, merchants, and students. Asian entry into Canada would be restricted to
the ports of Victoria and Vancouver.

The Chinese Exclusion Act proved to be very effective in halting
Chinese immigration. From the time the law was enacted in 1923 to the
time it was repealed in 1947, only 15 Chinese immigrants were admitted
into Canada. Wives and children of men already in the country were
denied entry. With no prospect of marriage on this side of the Pacific,
some men made the return trip to China. Others found themselves
trapped by a law that proved to be cruel and inhumane. Wayson Choy
in his book, *The Jade Peony*, wrote:

*"Poverty-stricken bachelor-men were left alone in Gold Mountain with
only a few dollars left to send back to China every month, and never enough*

dollars to buy passage home. Dozens went mad; many killed themselves. The Chinatown Chinese called July 1st, the day celebrating the birth of Canada, the Day of Shame." (p.17)

The act passed into law July 1st, 1923, coinciding with the celebration of Dominion Day, the anniversary of Canadian Confederation. It was such an insult that many Chinese refused to participate in Dominion Day events for many years, also referring to the day as "Humiliation Day."

Little realizing the challenges and obstacles that lay ahead, Eng Wing, a young man with the patience of an ox and dreams of a better life began his family. May 4th of 1914, The Year of the Tiger, Lin gave birth to their first son.

The Reverend Smith Stanley Osterhout, Methodist Superintendent of Oriental Missions for Western Canada from 1911 to 1939, was Pastor, mentor and long-time friend of the Wing family. (Photo – Kamloops Museum & Archives #1839)

Funeral in Kamloops' Chinatown, circa 1905
(photo – Kamloops Museum & Archives #5022)

Kamloops' Chinatown as seen from the Thompson River circa 1905
(photo – Kamloops Museum & Archives #5050)

This Kamloops, B.C. cemetery is the oldest known Chinese cemetery in Canada. The stone lions keep vigil over those souls that never returned to China. (photos – author)

The Silver Grill circa 1930 was originally the American Café. Note the living quarters above. (Kamloops Museum & Archives #6587)

Chapter 2

YEAR OF THE TIGER

A child's life, a piece of paper on which every person leaves a mark. (Chinese Proverb)

On May 4, 1914 in the Year of the Tiger on the Chinese calendar, Lin gave birth to her first child in a small nursing station maintained in a private residence. Dr. Stanley Osterhout, superintendent of the Methodist Mission, baptised the infant "Peter Wing." The happy parents brought their baby boy to their small home on the 300 block of Lansdowne Street. The house had two bedrooms, a living room and a kitchen. A wood cook stove in the kitchen and a potbelly stove in the living room were the extent of appliances. Peter and his future brothers and sisters – John, James, David, May, Lily and Jean – would eventually share one bedroom. The living room doubled as a third bedroom as the children grew older. There was no sense of privacy or of individual property. This practise of frugality and communal living sustained the family through two world wars and the Great Depression. It would also evidence itself in Peter's later public service and in his commitment to Eng and Lin in their old age.

The house on Lansdowne, along with The Good Eats restaurant and an occasional trip to the mission, was little Peter's world. Chinese was the language of the family. Public radio did not exist and the invention of television was years away.

With little sister May arriving fifteen months after Peter, there was little time for the joys of motherhood. Lin had her hands full with the running of the household.

"Mother told me, one time she came from the mission with me on a sled and by the time she got to the Hudson Bay there was nobody on the sled," recalled Peter. *"She had to come back to find me. I had fallen off."*

A local museum curator adds that Lin found Peter happily playing on the railway tracks that ran down the middle of Victoria Street, Kamloops' main thoroughfare.

"Dad had the restaurant before mother came," said Peter. *"So I was in and out of the restaurant as soon as I was able to walk…. One or two of the partners that dad had came from the same village so they considered themselves 'uncles'… and dad encouraged me to learn as much as I could. In those days anybody that was able of helping… washing dishes, peeling potatoes… everything had to be done. The cook that was responsible for bread and pastry had to start at three o'clock in the morning. I'm still using the same piecrust I learned then. We have a reputation of making the best piecrust in the whole town. The recipe doesn't count. It's just how you're able to work it out."*

Peter confided to me that the secret was extra lard. When he learned the recipe, the lard was rendered at home and then brought to the restaurant. Incidentally, he was still making pies in his 8os. I tried one and it was great!

"The soup stock was made from any bones that were available. They were thrown into a big pot," said Peter. *"About once a week a pig farmer came around and picked up all the scraps and hauled them away in a great big horse drawn cart. The scraps were put into another big boiler and fed to the pigs. Nothing was wasted. There is no word for 'garbage' in China."*

Peter learned early that you work to live and live to work. Every family member took part in the family business. His first job as a little boy was breaking up lumps of coal for the kitchen ranges at the restaurant. Today it is hard to imagine a coal-fired grill. The best chefs regulated their cooking temperatures by knowing the hot and warm spots on the grill and using them accordingly. Peter's other duties included washing dishes and peeling potatoes. Twice a week he arrived at 3:00 a.m. to assist the bread maker. His two "uncles" behaved more like bosses and made sure he always had plenty to do. Nothing on the menu was ready-made and nothing was wasted. The Wings understood "recycling" long before the word was in vogue.

Family meals consisted of traditional stir-fried Chinese vegetables. Bok choy, "white vegetable," is a bitter vegetable somewhat similar to romaine lettuce; sui choy, "crispy vegetable," is known as Chinese cabbage; and gai choy, "chicken vegetable," resembles Swiss chard. When unavailable, cabbage and other western vegetables sufficed. The family only ate rice that came from China in 20-kilogram straw bags tied with bamboo.

When Peter was about two years old, Eng had entered partnership in a general store and grocery, his third business venture. He was constantly looking for ways to advance the family and generally developing businesses that were essential to community needs. Eventually this would lead to real estate investments. It seems his decisions were made as a way to provide security for his family in a society that in many ways was hostile to his race. This would have a definite bearing on the upbringing of his children, which brings us back to Peter.

There were few toys in the Wing household, but Peter recalled being exposed to a succession of new and different playthings through the store,

"The way we had to run our household, we just didn't have any time for what you might call 'niceties'. There was always some kind of toys. If not available at home, I could always go to the store and enjoy them. We were never allowed to keep any toys. I enjoyed anything mechanical and I was able to look after anything that required assembly. The main thing I

remember about the house, it had a garage off the lane. Our store had a delivery truck and I was there more than anywhere else. I always was fascinated by anything mechanical."

In some ways Peter's childhood was more enriched than that of other children his age. This may explain his later "hands-on" approach toward work and toward life in general.

The restaurant acted as Peter's first window to the world. Beginning with the restaurant and more so with the grocery business that followed, everyone in Kamloops came to know the service-oriented young man named Peter Wing. Eng's decisions in operating the restaurants and later, the grocery, made the Wings a part of the community. The family was well-known and appreciated for the services they provided.

This does not mean that everyone in Kamloops was appreciative of its Chinese residents. Before World War I most resident Chinese in British Columbia operated small farms, sold produce door-to-door or operated small hand laundries. During the Great War many filled the vacuum left by young whites that enlisted in the armed forces. Returning veterans were not happy with the results. A hostile editorial in the *Kamloops Standard Sentinel* of 1917 reads, "Kamloops has no need of a commercial Chinese quarter... (we should) confine this detrimental movement to one part of the city. The salvation of prosperity in Kamloops is the prosperity of a white Kamloops and a white Kamloops district."

Such attitudes prevailed as Peter enrolled in the Stuart Wood School in the fall of 1920. He spoke no English and had the company of only five or six other Chinese children. Like all little children, Peter headed off to school with a mixture of fear and excitement at this new adventure. However, this little Chinese-speaking boy could hardly have been prepared to face "Chinka, chinka, Chinaman..." and "Peter, Peter, pumpkin eater...." Initially the language barrier was a blessing, but Peter came to loath these and other racist jingles. This was a part of growing up "Chinese."

"We were the only Chinese family not living in Chinatown in those days," said Peter. *"There was prejudice. There was no way of getting away from*

that. We had some rough racist kids. The bad ones, not bad, but inclined that way, that's where we had the most problems. We just sort of expected it. Our elders trained us to try to ignore that sort of thing because we were making our living off them. We just had to take a certain amount of that. And anyway, I was bigger than most of them, but it was hard. I was lucky in being associated with the church kids. They were really good friends and in the back of our minds we never felt ostracized."

Kim, Peter's wife who grew up in Revelstoke, British Columbia, added, *"We were used to it. You never knew when they would appear or where they would appear. Our parents always taught us, 'You never fight back!'"*

There was no recourse for these immigrant children. Their tormentors were children of people from whom their parents made their livelihood. It was crucial that they take the insults and walk away. No wonder so many from that generation seem to be such "quiet" people to those who do not understand.

Nonetheless, Peter loved school with its gifts of language, friendship and books. His best friend was Victor Arduini. Victor's father owned the shoemaker's shop next door to the Wing's restaurant and the two boys grew up together. Initially Victor spoke only Italian and Peter spoke only Chinese, so play had some challenges. The two boys eventually entertained senior citizens in the community with Victor playing the piano and Peter playing the violin. They also performed live in the early days of radio. Victor grew up to establish his own shoe store, Naturalizer Shoes, which remained in his family for many years. Like Peter, he was a second-generation immigrant who would establish himself and his family as part of the fabric of the community.

In a time not dominated by consumerism or television, children observed the activities around them and then created their own toys or shared the toys of others. Most games involved some social interaction and cooperation. A popular game of the time was played by tying two pieces of rubber cut from an old inner tube or tire on opposite ends of an eight-to-ten-inch string and then passing or throwing them with a stick from one child to another in a manner similar to lacrosse

(Canada's official national game). Other games still played today included marbles, hopscotch and jacks.

Outside of school, many hours were spent at the Methodist Chinese Mission. According to Peter, the mission set the stage for the success of the Chinese people in Kamloops. It was established in 1890, just two years after the Methodist church had opened its doors. In 1896, a Chinese Christian businessman died of tuberculosis, leaving his store to become the Chinese Mission Hall. This humble hall was like a second home to Peter. This is where Peter performed his first act of public service. He and May, his younger sister, cut down a Christmas tree for a church play.

The mission director, Dr. Osterhout, had worked in the missions of Canton. He spoke Chinese and was a guiding light to Peter and the other immigrant children. Through the mission they were introduced first to the church and then to the community at large. Dr. Osterhout later performed their weddings and baptised their children. During his lifetime he was always a friend and counsellor to the Wing family and highly respected by Peter personally.

"As soon as dad thought I was able, he arranged for me to have a few piano lessons," said Peter. *"I would go to the teacher to learn on the piano and then go to the mission to play on the pump organ. I got my love for singing from Dr. Osterhout. He had a beautiful bass voice. As soon as I could I joined the choir in the church."*

Peter's first hymnal, written in Chinese characters, could be seen on the electric organ in his home until 1998 when the organ was donated to the Kamloops United Church. As a boy he also learned violin and often performed with May Cheong, a missionary's daughter, who accompanied him on the organ. This music ministry continued until the mission closed in the 1940s. Peter sometimes filled in for the United Church organist and occasionally led the worship. He said that he missed this in his later years, *"I used to lead the hymns and now I can't sing because I can't see."*

A great deal of credit must be given to Peter's father. It seems that Eng took every opportunity to position the family, and Peter specifically, in activities that would lead to respect and acceptance as residents within Kamloops. Lacking the protection of citizenship, security of the family seemed to be in property and community service. Two decades later the Japanese in Canada would find this was not true.

The Wing family fortunes were growing. In 1916, Eng and his partners had purchased the property at 258 Victoria Street and opened The City Cash Grocery. This general store was the first of its kind in the community, "cash and carry." The norm for merchants of the time was to establish and carry a credit tab with customers throughout the year. It worked well for farmers, loggers and miners who could receive necessary supplies in the spring or fall and pay their tabs at the end of their respective seasons. Fishermen on the coast used the same system. Since store owners kept the only record of purchases and prices, this credit system often insured that customers remained in perpetual debt to the local store, reminiscent of the old coal mining song lyric, "I owe my soul to the company store." As one fisherman was heard to say, "I picked up my gear each spring and had to return one boot each fall." Eng offered the option of payment upon pick-up or delivery, freeing his patrons from a perpetual debt relationship to the store and freeing the store from the problems associated with collection.

It may be that Eng's view of personal debt came with him from China where every New Year each person was expected to make every effort to pay off old debts. It was not rare in the old Chinese tradition for men to resort to stealing in order to pay off debts and save their reputations (providing they didn't get caught, of course). In China, store owners were known to sell merchandise at sacrificial prices just before the Chinese New Year in order to square their debts. Sounds a little like Boxing Day sales in our time. The principle was to begin each year with a clean slate on which could be written a year of better success and greater happiness.

Sylvia Whalley, a long-time resident of Kamloops, shared a cute anecdote she received from her mother, one of the store's patrons. Her mother related going to the store and staring into a bin of tofu. A little boy named Peter looked at her and said, *"You won't like it."*

The store's 1913 Model T delivery van introduced Peter to what became a lifelong interest and hobby, automobiles. When at home his favourite pastime was examining the Model T. It is not hard to imagine a little boy sitting behind the steering wheel, grunting car sounds, and shifting levers and gears. The simple yet mysterious Model T motor begged to be examined.

"My most enjoyable activity was fiddling with mechanical things, mainly cars," said Peter. *"I would have looked into flying, but couldn't pass the vision exam."*

In time, Peter maintained all the family vehicles. Eng lived by the principle that you don't pay others to do what you can do for yourself. (And if you can't do it yourself, have your son take another course.) Peter was brought up with a "hands-on" philosophy that served him well in business and later in public service.

With the store providing a needed community service and the van doing the deliveries, the Wing family was viewed more favourably than the seasonal Chinese labourers of Chinatown. They were becoming part of the community, sharing both a vested interest and a commitment to the well-being of the town.

"As soon as I was old enough to understand the language and able to interpret I was pretty well into the adult world," said Peter. *"From age nine [dad] always took me to Vancouver twice a year for buying trips. His eyesight was rather poor. I read the street signs and went to the different wholesale buildings that he had to visit to do his purchasing."*

Peter became indispensable to the family business. At age nine, he climbed aboard a railway coach with his father and made the first of many trips to the growing city of Vancouver. This opened an exciting new world to his developing mind. Traveling down the Fraser River Canyon he experienced the reverse of Eng's trip of 1901. He must have marvelled at the river rapids rumbling to the coast. Perhaps there was a little fear as the train clung to the cliffs and he viewed the massive slides of rock blown away for placement of the rails. There was the shock and surprise of instant darkness as they hurdled through the tunnels. And the speed! Who would have imagined traveling at 35 miles per hour! The grades and tracks wouldn't allow for much more and sometimes required less. Could he have known of the sacrifice of Chinese labourers giving their lives for Canadian unity? An estimated one man per mile of track lost his life in constructing the rails. There was no compensation for their families, and wives and children were rarely notified.

Inside, the rhythmic clatter of the rails, the wailing of the whistle, the murmur of people meeting and greeting and the comments of the porter all came together like a grand locomotive overture. Air conditioning was synonymous with an open window. Fresh air included cinders and ash from the engine. Mind your eyes. Some, like Eng and Peter, shared a bag lunch. Others enjoyed the dining car. Men talked. Ladies read. Children cried. Farmers, ranchers, businessmen, tourists and families made their way together through the rainforests of Hope, past the lush farms and dairies of the Fraser Valley and into the frenetic scramble of Vancouver. Travel by train was a wonder!

Father and son always stayed at the Pennsylvania Hotel at the corner of Hastings and Carrall, just on the edge of Vancouver's Chinatown. Never having managed a good command of English, the rare cup of tea along with a hearty conversation about business in the new world and politics in the old would be rare pleasures for Eng. For Peter every new experience was a window to a larger world. Ever at his father's side, he read the street signs, double-checked the orders and interpreted important conversations dealing with business. These were major excursions for Peter.

Eng understood the need for some recreation and in 1925 took Peter on his first visit of many to the Pacific National Exhibition in Vancouver. The exhibition, which started in 1910, had become the second largest fair in North America, second only to the New York State Fair. Arriving by streetcar, father and son entered a showcase of technology and amusement. Scientific, industrial and agricultural exhibits promoted the latest in goods and technology. The exhibition showcased the latest creations of Henry Ford, which the American Automobile Association put to the test on the exhibition raceway. Enormous barns housed the

finest livestock in western Canada. Vancouver was well into developing "Happyland," a permanent amusement complex on the grounds.
Nightly fireworks and circus-like performances contributed to a wonderland of human progress. It seems the ever-practical Eng was always
looking for new ideas and innovations and was purposely exposing
Peter to experiences that would later be applied in business and community service.

Just as the Wings felt they were making progress in being assimi-
lated into the community, the harsh reality of their true position was
made amply clear on Dominion Day, July 1, 1923 when the Chinese
Exclusion Act took effect. Because of their association with the church,
the school and patrons of the family business, they had not felt like out-
siders in the community. Eng had always encouraged family acknowl-
edgement of the Dominion Day events. Would he now emphasize the
date as "Humiliation Day" and boycott the celebration along with
many other immigrants or continue participation as usual? This man of
few words and great plans must have been confident that "time always
turns," that the time of the *Chinese Canadian* would yet come. In the
meantime, his family would continue to quietly observe the national
holidays as though the time had already arrived.

*"Our family wasn't concerned about [the Exclusion Act], but most of
the Chinese community was,"* explained Peter. *"They didn't like to see us
participate in the May Day celebrations or the first of July celebrations."* So
why participate? *"We were part of the community. More of our friends
were Caucasian than Chinese."*

Like most children, Peter and his siblings were unaware of the
social issues facing their parents. Their first responsibility was school
and after that, helping in the store. At the Stuart Wood School Peter
was second tallest in his class and generally appeared and acted older
than his peers. Since he excelled in academics, his teachers moved him
from grade 6 straight to grade 9. He continued to excel, but toward
the end of 1927 began experiencing chronic fatigue. His joints ached
and he suffered recurrent fevers. Eng and Lin were concerned about a
general weight loss in their son. Each symptom pointed to a different

illness. The only thing the doctor could prescribe was long-term rest with plenty of sleep and no stress. The illness was never diagnosed. Taking all the prevalent symptoms into account and considering a full year of recovery, Peter probably suffered from mononucleosis or rheumatic fever.

What does a 13-year-old do when confined to bed in the year 1927?

"I was very fortunate," explained Peter. *"The Sunday school teacher, Mr. Taylor, operated a bookstore. He kept me in books all the time I was in and out of the hospital."*

Mr. Taylor loaned Peter classics such as *Tom Sawyer* and *Huckleberry Finn* by Mark Twain. Other classics of the time would have included books like *Little Women* and *Little Men* by Louisa May Alcott and *Black Beauty* by Anna Sewell. Taylor, whether by design or by chance, was subtly molding the thoughts and opinions of Peter by also bringing the latest books on world travel and anthropology, reasonably advanced reading for a 13-year-old. Peter recalled no specific titles, but remembered being introduced to the writing of Margaret Mead. Her first book, *Coming of Age in Samoa,* was a bestseller published during Peter's convalescence. This anthropological study of youth, specifically of adolescent girls, seems like an odd contribution by a Sunday school teacher. Mead became one of Peter's favourite authors and he shared her views on Christian missionaries and primitive cultures. He quickly pointed out that many cultures had operative religions hundreds of years before Christianity. Like Meade, he believed that Christianity should never have been forced on indigenous cultures, an interesting view since he himself was a devoted Christian.

Reading and sleeping have their limits, so what else can a young teen do when confined to the house?

Peter continued, *"That was when radios came in and dad was fortunate enough to have the money to buy a radio. I began logging radio stations."*

It was probably with Peter in mind that Eng purchased the family's first radio in 1927. Scanning the airways became an imaginative way of travel and adventure that took Peter beyond what was taught in school or found in books. Soon he was logging the different stations. Between his books and the radio, he developed a broad world-view. Ideas about people, cities, culture and government were being planted that would later bear fruit in public service and city government.

Radio broadcasting had only begun around 1920 and the first vacuum tube radios did not reach the market until 1924. What began as a novelty was gradually becoming a mass medium. There were only about sixty radio stations across Canada compared to hundreds across the United States. Networks were in their infancy and most stations hosted local programing, had low power and short broadcast range. Eighty percent of the programing was American and already there was concern about the American threat to Canadian culture. The first Kamloops station (CFJC) made its initial broadcast in October of 1926 with 15 watts of power and a range of about 2400 kilometres (1500 miles). In the truest sense it was "local" radio. Music was broadcast live or from phonograph records. The few shows that existed, such as *Sam 'n Henry* in the States, were distributed on vinyl recordings. To own a radio was a luxury and often families and neighbours gathered together to listen to favourite programs. So how did Peter manage to log more than local Kamloops radio?

First, all radios of the time required antennas, the better the antenna, the better the range of reception. Peter would have quickly learned that antenna wires strung throughout his room were inefficient. He needed an antenna running up the side of the house, or better yet across the roof or on a tower similar to later television antennas. This still offered only better reception of local radio and little radius for other stations. What he soon discovered was the existence of what is called the radio "bounce" or "skip."

This "bounce" can extend a broadcast range by thousands of kilometres as sound waves "bounce" off the atmospheric ionosphere back to earth. Peter probably didn't know that the ionosphere is a layer of the earth's atmosphere that contains a high concentration of ions and free electrons that reflect radio signals back to earth, but he certainly benefited from it. Strong radio signals can actually bounce two or more times. This "bounce" is most effective at night when the ionosphere is at its thickest. Because of sunspot activity reception can vary anywhere from a minute to several hours. The challenge for Peter was in getting the call letters and location of a station before losing reception. There was often frustration at losing an interesting program before hearing its conclusion. Imagine a good radio mystery fading out just before the climax. Sometimes changing the position of the antenna could pick it back up. Most times it could not!

Radio was a nighttime activity. Peter invented other pastimes for the day.

"I would have a contest with myself. If I heard a car go by, I would say, 'Oh, that's Dr. Burris' car,' or 'that's Dr. Willoughby's car.' I got so I could recognize every car that went by."

Sometimes his mother, Lin, would confirm his guess or Peter would take a quick glance out the window for verification. At the time, the immediate population of Kamloops was under 6,000 people. The majority were still driving horses or travelling by foot. Peter estimated that there were only fifty or sixty cars in the local community. Most were owned by doctors, lawyers or cab drivers. He could identify every car in the area by its engine sound.

As the New Year came around, Peter's health improved. He was only 14 years old, but his regular school days were over. For him, teenage as experienced today would never exist. The economic needs of the family required that he take his place in the family business. This was not uncommon for young men in the 1920s and 1930s.

While Peter was still convalescing, the Fraser Canyon Highway from Vancouver to Kamloops was completed. Eng, in keeping up with the times, purchased a Model T roadster for the family, but did not feel comfortable driving because of his poor eyesight. The roads were poor at best and hazardous for anything faster than a horse and the Model T was prone to jackknife with the front wheels flipping from right to left and back when inexperienced drivers jerked the steering wheel.

An elderly miner from northwestern Ontario explained the risky steering by relating an occasion when he, as a teen, joined his friends for a joyride in a Model T. When their driver lost control and began zigzagging down the road at top speed (thirty miles an hour?), the rest of the group bailed out. The driver, discovering he was by himself, stood up and leapt from the car too. With the old hand throttle, the Model T wouldn't have stopped until it ran out of gas or collided with ... whatever. Such sport was great for silent movies, but not for the average family. The Model T was great for getting around town, but not ideal for cross-country trips.

Eng quickly traded the Model T for a new 1928 Chevrolet sedan and arranged for Peter to obtain a driver's license. From that time Eng had the wheels and the driver necessary for both business and his one recreational pleasure, fishing at Paul Lake, about 20 miles north of Kamloops. It seems that fishing, with its practical benefits, well-suited Eng's work ethic.

By the fall of 1929, Eng had a new business in mind which required his son's full-time involvement, but first Peter was enrolled in the Special Commercial Class offered at the local high school. This was the equivalent of taking a certificate or diploma program through a local college today. The class emphasized accounting and typing. Peter left the school in March of 1930 when the Cut Rate Self-Serve Grocery opened. What he had learned in class, he now put to use in business. Eng provided the practical setting to learn firsthand and the progressive approach to always be moving forward. Peter's first job was running the mimeograph machine to produce fliers advertising the weekly specials. People needed to know what they were selling and that their store was the best place to shop. With the fliers came even greater innovations.

Peter explained, *"Most grocery stores just had bins of different things and you bought half a pound or a pound or a dollar's worth or something like that. We were the first store to pre-package our stock."*

Eng and his partners had already introduced the idea of "cash and carry." They now extended this by pre-packaging the goods in the commonly ordered amounts (half- pound, pound, etc.). Small wire baskets were made available for customers to "shop" their own lists. Delivery was still available, but now there was a 10-cent delivery fee. This was the first store in Kamloops with pre-packaged goods that customers could pick out for themselves. Competition came the following year with the Overwaitea Grocery Store moving in next door and Safeway not far behind, but it was the Wings who brought "cash and carry" and "self-serve" to Kamloops.

Eng Wing's management style was slightly different from traditional Chinese ways. In Chinese society, social and political organisation was based on the family, with the father bearing the responsibility for the moral quality and views of all family members. Eng, however, recognised his own limitations.

"Dad considered me as superior because I could speak fluent English," said Peter. *"He would discuss decisions with all of us. He knew his limits and he set us standards. Then we had to adapt what he knew to conditions that were current."*

Success demanded that the family move forward together. By the end of 1930 Peter worked full-time in the store. He was 16 years old, six foot one inch tall and eager to help build the family fortunes. In recalling his early experiences, Peter said he was never a *"wannabe."* He did not have predetermined goals or seek positions for the sake of prestige. It seemed that people around him pointed out jobs that needed to be done and encouraged him to do them. In an interview with *Kamloops This Week*, January 10, 1993, Peter commented, *"Each thing I got involved with was a necessity at the time. Then it would be time to move on."* He always referred to himself as a *"hands-on expert,"* willing to try any job, but always learning from the ground up. This especially pertained to the family business.

An example of this is seen in the Wing purchase of the property currently occupied by the Scotiabank on the corner of 3rd and Victoria Street in Kamloops. The family store was on the main level with bachelor suites situated in the upper story. Provincial regulations required certified maintenance for the manually stoked steam furnace. An engineer was needed on site until automatic stokers were introduced in the mid-1930s.

"As soon as I was old enough I applied for a steam engineer's certificate," said Peter. *"As I understand it, I was the* second *Chinese in British Columbia to receive a steam engineer's ticket."*

Plumbing and electrical maintenance for the family holdings became Peter's responsibility. In fact, when the Wing Building, located at the same intersection, was constructed in the late 1940s, Peter installed at least half the wiring. *"The only jobs that I didn't try to do were brick laying and plastering."*

Though much of Peter's life was directed by family needs, his advice to young people:

"Find a line of business or a profession you really enjoy and follow it through. Don't aim at the sky, but do a good job with whatever you are doing. The rewards will follow. Girls, get your education!"

As Peter approached his late teens, the time had come for the family to find a suitable bride. His first meeting with the girl who was to become his lifelong partner came through an unexpected request from a family in Revelstoke, British Columbia.

Chapter 3

BEAM OF LIGHT

*Simple to open a shop, another thing
to keep it open. (Chinese Proverb)*

Peter repeatedly stated that his accomplishments would have been impossible without the support and encouragement of his wife, Kim. Her family name, "Kwong," translated as "Beam of Light" or "Brightness," readily describes her contribution to the Wing family.

The Kwongs were from the merchant class of Chinese society. Kim's grandfather was a Chinese herbalist doctor. Wong, her father, was a merchant. His coming to Canada and the involvement of the Kwongs in Revelstoke and other parts of British Columbia are significant.

Wong Kwong landed in Victoria in 1899. Being of hefty stature he immediately began work for the Canadian Pacific Railroad. The railroad had reached the Pacific Ocean and was focusing on the development of bridges and tunnels through the mountains. One major operational improvement was construction of the Spiral Tunnels, needed to reduce a hazardous grade in the Kicking Horse Pass. The other was construction of the Connaught Tunnel in the Roger's Pass, needed to avoid the massive winter avalanches of the Rocky Mountains. Since Wong was well-educated, he was a natural choice as foreman of a Chinese construction gang. The CPR sent him to the Connaught Tunnel project outside of Revelstoke, British Columbia, a tunnel running eight kilometres (five miles) through Mount McDonald and the longest tunnel in the Western Hemisphere at the time.

Credit for the very existence of Revelstoke must be given to the trans-continental rail system. As the divisional point between Calgary and Vancouver, Revelstoke was an important stop for the trains. It was named after Lord Revelstoke, head of the British banking firm of Baring Brothers, which purchased a considerable share of the first bond issue of the Canadian Pacific Railroad.

Revelstoke is also known as a fishing and hunting paradise. The headwaters of the Columbia River are near there. The Arrow Lakes, part of the Columbia River system, make for fabulous fishing and canoeing. Just outside the town, Mount Revelstoke, with an elevation of 7,000 feet, beckons hikers to an alpine wonderland of wild flowers and mountain grandeur. Grizzly bears are regular residents in the area and a sheep bell on a hiker's belt is thought to be a good safety precaution, though it has been said that bear cubs will sometimes be drawn to the sound out of curiosity and bring mama bear along. Most people agree that the bruins prefer to avoid confrontation with people, but when cornered or disturbed, they are deadly!

Wong immediately saw the need for support facilities for the rail workers. To this end he established a boarding house and an Asian import store for Oriental foods and supplies. Since Wong could read and write both Cantonese and English, guest workers looked to him to write letters to their families in China and to advise them in financial and business matters in Canada. He was also an apt translator when called upon.

An ancient Hebrew proverb says, "…make it fit for thyself in the field; and afterward build thine house" (Proverbs 24:27). Like other Chinese immigrants planning to stay in North America, Wong first established his business and then in 1907 returned to China to take a wife. The family choice was Yee Von, a young woman from the village of Hoi Sun in Canton. Yee had been raised and prepared for marriage into the upper class, a testimony to Wong's family status in China.

The place of a woman in the Chinese family should be noted. Every woman was to be subject to the "three obediences"- obedience to the father, obedience to the husband and obedience to the eldest son. In reality, the mother often ruled the home and Chinese women were frequently of excellent business capacity, which certainly proved true with Yee.

Regarding class distinctions, Kim said, *"Once we were in Canada, everybody was the same."*

Peter added, *"Kim's father had rooms upstairs in his store for boarders. And for a short time he had a sawmill too. The Kwongs were left over from the old construction gangs. They moved to Edmonton for a short time, but they found the winters too rough there so they came back to Revelstoke."*

The winters must have been exceptionally bad in Edmonton, because in Revelstoke the Kwongs sometimes used the upstairs windows to get in and out of the house during the winter because of the snow.

Yee suffered one major handicap. As a baby her feet had been tightly bound to prevent their natural growth. Each foot, called Gin Lien (Golden Lilly or Golden Lotus), was less than four inches long. The result was severe deformity and lifelong crippling. As early as the 10th or 11th centuries Lotus Feet were considered a mark of aristocratic beauty and ensured marriage into the upper class, which also meant confinement to the home. Other women worked the fields, served as domestics or lived as concubines. The custom continued in parts of China until the 1930s. In spite of this handicap, Yee bore five girls and four boys to the Wong family. Her greatest contribution to Canada came through her children.

Yee was well-educated in the customs of Old China. The New Moon festival and the Chinese New Year were big family events for the Kwongs. The New Moon Festival each fall celebrated the gathering of crops and family, thanksgiving for the harvest, and prayer for long life and a good future. Yee prepared the special moon cakes, which Wong cut into pieces and the children delivered to the workers at the family boarding house.

During the Chinese New Year Yee prepared the traditional dumplings made from flour, lean pork, green onions, lotus root and ginger. Formed in the shape of ancient Chinese currency, these were eaten to bring wealth in the coming year. Random dumplings were stuffed with coins, candy, peanuts or chestnuts: the coins signifying wealth; the candy portending sweetness of life; the peanuts symbolizing health and longevity; the chestnuts promising vitality and vigour. These were shared with the boarders and must have been very special treats. These men had arrived in Canada just as railway construction was winding down, too late to harvest the imagined money trees of the *Gold Mountain* and too poor to return to their homeland. Many were reduced to cooking and waiting tables in the local restaurants. The concern of the Kwongs must have been precious indeed.

Homesick and lonely men were often temporarily adopted into the Kwong family. Kim said, *"There were so many bachelors and mother would mend their slacks and make shirts for them."*

Yee was basically housebound, but *"she did a lot of sewing."*

Peter expressed the highest and possibly inflated regard for his mother-in-law, *"Kim's mother and her reputation for service in Revelstoke… well, she didn't speak English… if her mother hadn't had bound feet… but she just wasn't able to move around… she could have been Mayor if she wanted."*

Kim had great memories of growing up in Revelstoke, *"All the kids were about the same age and were just one big family. After school we used to play in the alley. There would be two whole baseball teams. Some of the ladies came out too, before they cooked supper. We had lots of fun that way.*

"Our mother was very capable. We lost our father when we were just young kids. That's how we learned to look after ourselves, which was very good. We were all close together that way and took care of one another. We

didn't say, 'Who's going to cook the meal?' Everybody put a hand to it and it was easy."

Wong had foreseen that completion of the railway would lead to less and less revenue from the store and boarding house. As the family grew, he started the Kwong Lee Laundry, which served the larger community and provided better financial security for his wife and children.

Laundries in the 1930s were much more labour intensive than today. The Kwong children started work in the morning before going to school, worked during the noon break and returned to work after school. The laundry operation often continued until 11 or 12 o'clock at night – seven days a week. The main customer was Revelstoke's Regent Hotel, which paid 1 cent per laundered bed sheet. The washing machine for the hotel sheets and tablecloths was an immense revolving barrel powered by a gasoline motor. Mechanical wringers were turned by hand and an open-walled shed had been constructed for natural air-drying. A mangle consisting of two large sheets of metal had been fabricated for ironing the hotel sheets and tablecloths. This particular mangle had to be five or six feet wide, because it could press an entire sheet without any folding being necessary. All other laundry was washed by hand in a wood-heated clothes boiler and ironed with heavy flat irons that were heated on an old coal stove. Deliveries were made by horse.

Kim commented, *"We never had a social life. As soon as I got home from school I was working. The boys would go out with the horse and deliver the laundry and the girls would be at home helping with ironing and whatever."*

The Kwong children were popular. Friends often joined them while they worked and sometimes helped. One of Kim's friends was called "the Chinese blonde" because she spent so much time at their home. To have any child drop out of school to work in the business was never considered an option by Wong or Yee.

Kim said, *"My mother always said, 'If you're not educated you can't think straight and people won't listen to you.'"*

Like her brothers and sisters, Kim finished high school and was planning a nursing career when she met Peter. Yee's other children and grandchildren eventually included three nurses, two doctors, one lawyer, four engineers, one teacher, one pharmacist, two chartered accountants and one hospital administrator.

No doubt there was the occasional longing, if not the lustful glance, of a lonely boarder toward the Kwong daughters. By 1920 the Chinese male-female ratio in Canada was estimated at ten to one. Daughters were a rare and valuable commodity. Arranging marriage of a Kwong daughter to a temporary peasant labourer was not an option. Though practising many Chinese traditions within the home, the Kwongs maintained Christian beliefs and wanted Christian husbands for their daughters. They had no intention of their children returning to China. One tradition they kept was that marriage must be arranged by the parents. Arranging a Canadian-born husband for a Chinese daughter was not easy. It was even more difficult for families seeking Chinese wives for their sons. Families intent on establishing themselves in Canada networked with others throughout the Dominion. Wong and Yee had "New World" plans for their children and it would not be a world in which women's feet were bound and husbands might have more than one wife.

In early 1931, the Wings in Kamloops received a request for help from the Kwong family in Revelstoke. The Kwong's oldest son, Sam, had contracted tuberculosis and was confined to the King Edward Sanatorium in Tranquille just outside North Kamloops. Their daughters were coming to Kamloops by rail and needed transportation between the train station and the sanatorium.

"[Meeting Kim] was sort of a happy coincidence," said Peter. *"Her brother had contracted tuberculosis on a trip to China. Tranquille was a tuberculosis centre for Canada, so he became a patient there. I was the only Chinese person in Kamloops that had a private car, so when the three teenage girls came to visit their brother, it was a happy coincidence."*

This was a new and certainly enjoyable experience for Peter. At age 18, he had never dated. His life had been school, church and work. There were only five Chinese families in Kamloops and no marriageable girls. Dating as known today did not exist within the Chinese community and marriage outside ethnic lines was completely unacceptable in the 1930s.

Kim and her sisters found a trip to Kamloops more like a holiday than a hospital visit. For Peter, chauffeuring the three sisters was his closest experience to going on a date. When asked if there was a magic moment when Peter and Kim "knew" they were meant for each other, they both answered, "No." Romance was not part of Chinese culture and tradition. Parents arranged the marriages of their children and romance came after and not before.

"In those days nearly every Chinese in Canada had some connection with somebody else," explained Peter. *"So really it was just one big family of 25 or 35,000 people. That's all there were. There was some correspondence between all families throughout Canada from Halifax to Vancouver.*

"Our [young] people had no real social life anyway. As soon as the eldest in the family gets to the [right] age, the family from all around start to encourage [marriage]. We never thought anything different about it. We never thought of courtship as we understand it today. Basically everything was set up by the family. I didn't know enough about the language to even use the word "love" as some people do. The integrity of the family and the strength of family ties were more important than what we in North America call 'love.' [Television and radio promote the idea that] sex is love and it isn't.

"My parents actually had contacted other families and we did have one of the girls come and visit with us for awhile. But [Kim and I] happened to meet at the right time. I think fate or God had something to do with it. It worked out wonderfully."

Peter was sent to Revelstoke to meet Wong and Yee. Because the Wings came from the peasant class of China whereas the Kwongs came from the merchant class, such contact would not have taken place in China, but both families had come to Canada looking for a new and different life. Yee had taught her children, *"... in Canada everybody is the same. They don't do that over here, so we don't have to."*

Peter was the only Wing to see the girls' father. Wong was recovering from a stroke when Peter first met him in Revelstoke. He died later the same summer.

With Wong's death the Kwong family faced a new reality: nine fatherless children ranging in age from 5 to 22 and a considerable family debt. Without Wong the family could no longer operate the Chinese store, which had functioned in Chinese for Chinese-speaking customers and stocked Chinese merchandise. Yee had all she could do with the children and they were not fluent in either the Chinese language or the Chinese culture. Major decisions had to be made immediately. Without the store, the laundry, which rarely brought in more than 30 dollars per month, became their primary support. Yee organised her children into a work unit that not only sustained the family, but also paid off considerable family debt and enabled several of the children to pursue higher education.

Peter, having just met the family, began travelling to Revelstoke.

"One of the first things I did was to keep their machinery going. We would go up every two or three weeks and fix whatever machine needed fixing. The greatest challenge was keeping the huge cumbersome belts on the washing machine in proper alignment."

With his aptitude for mechanics and his boiler certification, Peter was a natural for the job. The trip via what is now the old Vernon Highway took nearly six hours – one way. The same trip today on the Trans-Canada Highway takes a leisurely two and a half hours.

Before Wong's death, Jean and Kim, the two oldest daughters, had planned to study nursing. This was now financially impossible.

"At that time [Kim] and her sister had planned to go to the United States to study nursing," explained Peter. *"When this happened it changed the plans of the family and Kim's sister. [With] some influence from the local people in Revelstoke, [Jean] enrolled in the [local] hospital as an apprentice. Although it was a small hospital, it had what they called a "school of nursing." It took a lot of influence to do because at that time professions weren't encouraged [for the Chinese], but that's what happened."*

Jean was accepted into the program out of respect for the family. The residents of Revelstoke looked upon the Kwong family as one of their own even though the Dominion of Canada did not. Jean later finished her course at the Royal Columbian Hospital in New Westminster, the first nurse of Chinese ancestry to graduate in Canada.

Yee decided that Kim would be given in marriage. How the choice was made is not clear, but she was determined to take care of her children. By Chinese tradition the oldest child should marry first. In this case that was Sam. Jean, the oldest daughter, was intent upon nursing and Kim was third in line. Yee, the protector of tradition, made certain that special gifts were presented to Sam and Jean, annulling their rights as older siblings and ensuring a successful marriage for Kim.

"What we call dating today hardly ever happened among the Chinese of that day," explained Peter. *November 11ᵗʰ, 1931, I took the drive to Revelstoke via Enderby and around Mara Lake, about five hours each way. There were three girls within about four years of each other. That was one of the discussions we had with the family. Traditionally the oldest is supposed to marry before the younger ones, so there was kind of a ritual we had to go through. It was sort of a semi-religious ritual to insure fertility and this sort of thing.*

"God was sure looking down on us. I would never have gotten to the position I did without Kim."

The Kwong family 1927
(photo courtesy of Peter & Kim Wing)

**Peter Wing and Kim Kwong's wedding party, November 6, 1932
(photo courtesy Peter & Kim Wing)**

Chapter 4

SIDE BY SIDE

*In bed be wife and husband, in hall each
other's honoured guest. (Chinese Proverb)*

Peter and Kim were married November 6th, 1932 in the Kamloops
United Church. Doris, Kim's younger sister, stood as maid of honour.
The reception took place in the Chinese Mission. Once again, we see
the care and mentoring of Dr. Osterhout.

*"Our wedding was mainly Christian-Canadian style," said Peter. "We
had the Superintendent of Missions, Dr. Osterhout, the main preacher; Mr.
Dredge, the local preacher; Jimmy Kwong, sort of a 42nd cousin, [the best
man]. We were influenced by the Christian and Canadian way of life, but
we kept the parts of the Chinese that was practical without upsetting things.
I think it worked out very well."*

Between the Kwongs and Wings existed a unique mix of Chinese
and Canadian tradition. Within the Chinese family all members
have their place in proper order by age and generation. In China, this

principle of loyalty to one's own family was considered a basic principle of life.

As soon as the eldest child was of age, marriage was expected and encouraged by the entire extended family. The fundamental purpose of marriage was not love, but rather, the continuation and integrity of the family. The "bride price" was not looked on as the purchase of a wife, but rather, as a gift sealing the relationship between two families, a strong reason for arranged marriages. Romance had little meaning in such an important decision. Young people were taught, "wedding first, love afterwards." After marriage a young bride belonged to her husband's family and came under the authority of her mother-in-law. It was customary that grandparents play a large role in rearing the grandchildren. In common practise, grandparents, parents and children lived under the same roof. Possessions, earnings and expenses were shared. Though Peter and Kim claimed they were not bound by these traditions, we see these very customs enacted in their day-to-day lives and commitment to Peter's mother and father. Considering the cultural backgrounds of both the Wings and the Kwongs, this would certainly have seemed natural.

In the traditional wedding, the daughter-in-law served tea first to her new father-in-law and then to her new mother-in-law. Each of the new "parents," using both hands, then presented the new "daughter" with a package wrapped in red containing money and a piece of jewellery to ensure the endurance of a long and honourable relationship. With that the marriage was complete. The Wings opted for a more Canadian service.

The planned honeymoon was immediately delayed. With the stress and emotion associated with the wedding, Peter's mother suffered a severe attack of asthma and needed Peter and Kim's care. A week later the young couple began a long and fruitful marriage with a brief honeymoon on Vancouver Island. Peter's response to the old saying, "Behind every successful man stands a good woman" was:

"My wife stands beside me! When you have somebody behind you or with you, things go a lot easier. That's the way it went. She was always there. A good friend is the most valuable thing we can get!"

The couple lived with Eng and Lin in the house they had purchased in 1923, almost ten years earlier. Eng, always of a practical bent, had added the basement and bathroom. He now added a bedroom for Peter and Kim. Chinese tradition dictated that the eldest son live with his parents and that his wife come under their authority. Because of Lin's asthma and frail health, Kim soon ran the household, looking after her mother-in-law and helping with the children. Peter's youngest brother, David, was yet to be born, so in a very real sense the young Wings experienced parenthood in raising Peter's siblings. This arrangement lasted for the next eleven years.

Shortly after the wedding, Eng took the greater part of the family to Hong Kong, leaving Peter, Kim and Peter's sister, May, to run the business. Peter was only 19 years old. Kim and May were both 18. Eng may have been exploring the possibility of relocating the family. Enforcement of the Oriental Exclusion Act had effectively closed the immigration of Chinese into Canada. The lingering depression and economic hardship on all fronts served to increase anti-Asian sentiment and prejudice. "White Only" practises were affecting jobs and purchasing practises throughout British Columbia. When he returned to Canada in 1934, he asked Peter and Kim to join the others in Hong Kong where the couple stayed from May to December.

When Peter and Kim disembarked, the temperature was very similar to Kamloops, mid-nineties Fahrenheit, but the high subtropical humidity was oppressive. This would be compensated before their return with a mild, dry, sunny winter.

The British elegance and Chinese charm of Hong Kong must have been amazing. British liners and freighters shared the harbour with the colourful Chinese junks. Fish stalls with all the variety of the South Pacific rivalled anything the Wings had ever seen. Boatmen, fishermen, carters and merchants thronged the thoroughfares. Dozens of rickshaws stood ready to carry shoppers and tourists wherever they desired.

The city, with its three, four and five story buildings and hundreds of pedestrians was alive with sounds, smells and activity. Exploring the shops, examining the displays and haggling with the merchants rivalled anything Peter had seen at Vancouver's Pacific National Exhibition.

In Hong Kong Peter experienced a different form of prejudice from that of British Columbia. The colony maintained its own unique class system. A form of segregation barred Chinese from living in the elegant Victoria Park, which was reserved for Europeans. The British maintained exclusive racetracks, cricket and polo fields and an elite school to serve their own "kind." Upper class Chinese countered this with their own social exclusivism and an elite school for their "kind." The merchant middle class was open to the Wings through Kim's family. Below that, the working class provided a foundation to support the whole.

"One of Kim's uncles was a banker [and wanted us to stay there]," said Peter. *"We could read and write English and would have been quite an asset to them, [but] we had been brought up in the Canadian way of life. We had one servant [even though] mother didn't want servants. If you didn't have a servant [and went to the] market on your own, you'd get gypped right and left. The servant did the marketing for you. The only serious opportunity [I had] to leave Kamloops was Hong Kong, [but] we had been brought up in the Canadian way of life and Hong Kong just didn't seem right for us. I just couldn't stand [that] way of life."*

Though Peter grew up as part of a small minority in a British culture, the first time he genuinely felt out of place was in Hong Kong. His six foot one inch frame attracted far more attention among the Chinese than his racial roots ever attracted among Canadians. He recalled entering a shop to hear one attendant address the other in Cantonese, "There's a foreign devil! It's your turn. You serve him." Peter simply bided his time before bidding the clerk a good day in impeccable Cantonese.

Peter and Kim wanted to explore their family roots in Mainland China, but the political climate was highly unstable. Japan had invaded Manchuria in 1931 and was well-established in several northern Chinese provinces by 1933. Severe fighting was taking place between Nationalist China and the Red Army. The winds of World War II were growing. The family returned to Canada at the end of 1934. This decision turned out to be providential. Seven years later, December 25th, 1941, Sir Mark Young, the Governor of Hong Kong, surrendered the British Crown Colony to Imperial Japan. In the turmoil of the time Britain refused to evacuate non-British subjects. We can only conjecture what the Wing's would have faced.

With his family reunited in Canada, it seems that Eng once more looked for ways of protecting his children's future. Meanwhile Peter, as the eldest son, was expected to extend that future to the next generation, so the family rejoiced to learn that Kim was expecting, but the patter of little feet was not to be. The pregnancy ended with a difficult miscarriage and complications ended any hope for subsequent pregnancies. Their close friend, the Reverend Chow Ling of Vancouver, had faced the same situation in his own marriage and extended his personal experience and strength to Peter and Kim. Perhaps it was simply the Chinese way that enabled the Wings to put their disappointment aside.

Kim commented on this trial, *"We didn't [go through a long period of disappointment] because we just looked forward to life. If it was that way, we would just accept it. At the time, the minister – he was very good and had no children – said, 'Anything in life that comes, God wants it that way.'"*

Peter added, *"It was a disappointment, but it was to be and we wouldn't have accomplished what we did if we did have a family."*

Because of the private nature of the Wings, there were those in the community who circulated a quite different story explaining the childlessness of the couple. Local gossips conjectured that the Kwongs knew that Kim could not bear children long before Peter came into the picture. In order to secure her future, they therefore offered Eng Wing, Peter's father, a substantial dowry. As the story goes, Eng, facing desperate financial problems, made the transaction in order to save the family business. This story was pure fabrication and totally ignored the facts as well as the importance of children in the traditional Chinese family.

While Peter and Kim struggled to "just accept" their loss and move forward, Eng refused to "just accept" the insecurity brought on the Chinese and other immigrants by the Depression.

Chapter 5

THE GREAT DEPRESSION

*When a cup of water is needed in many
places at one time, life becomes difficult indeed. (Chinese Proverb)*

"In those days it was a struggle regardless of who you were," Peter emphasized. *"We were married in '32 and the Depression started to come out
around '30. We were pretty well on the right side of the hill at that time and
we were able to take advantage of what little was available for us and built
up from there. We never wanted for anything and we enjoyed a lot more
amenities than most people, but one thing my father instilled on us, 'Don't
get anything until you can pay for it.'"*

Before going to Hong Kong, the Wings must have considered the
possibility of losing everything as The Great Depression dragged into
the late 1920s and the early 1930s. The Depression had created a fearful
environment for the "guest" people from Asia, perhaps the greatest
threat coming from strong racial prejudice. Bigots, with their idea
that "everything would be all right if we just get rid of 'them,'" were

influencing business practises and public policy. Private ownership of land and business was a privilege given or taken at the discretion of the government. Every Asian business was required to obtain a government license to operate, whether it be a simple hand laundry or a door-to-door fruit and vegetable peddler. As early as 1919, the city of Kamloops had restricted Chinese laundries to the west end of the city, allowing only the all-white Kamloops Steam Laundry to operate in the city proper. Interestingly, the Kamloops Steam Laundry went out of business, because city residents were willing to travel to the west end of town for better prices. Chinese workers were accused of taking away badly needed jobs, which in some cases they did. They were willing to work for lower wages because they too badly needed jobs.

An editorial found in the *Kamloops Sentinel* exposes the inconceivable prejudice faced by the Chinese in the larger community:

"...Take the Chinese. Not one in one hundred will ever go back to China to live, and while they are growing up, educated at the expense of the white taxpayer, flocks of others are crowding over, entering into competition with the white races, absorbing jobs that might well come to our own immigrants. The late Sir Richard McBride is credited with saying that he had every admiration for the races of the Orient in their own countries. In their own countries, yes. Let them stay there...the time is ripe for the question of exclusion to be seriously tackled. South Africa, long incensed at Indian encroachment, has agreed with India upon a policy of repatriation. Australia is white and intends to remain so. The U.S. has an exclusion policy, to say nothing of a quota law for all immigrants. Shall B.C., shall Canada be the dumping ground?" ("Current Comment by Democratis" Editorial. Kamloops Sentinel March 4, 1927)

Imagine the rumours, stories and fear being spread within the Chinese community as the Klu Klux Klan embraced the cause of white anti-Asian prejudice. By 1927 Klan membership in British Columbia was around 13,000 and was flexing a degree of political muscle. The Klan presented a resolution to Kamloops City Council asking for the repatriation of all Asians and the confiscation of their properties within the municipality. City Council refused to endorse the resolution, but the vote was an alarming 3 to 2. Had it passed it likely would have been disallowed by the Province or the Dominion, but nonetheless, it was within the realm of possibility that Asians would find themselves as impoverished refugees seeking asylum in countries totally alien to their children who had been raised in Canada. It is no wonder Eng considered relocating the family to Hong Kong while he still controlled the family assets in Canada.

Eventually the Klan declined, but there is still a strong White Supremacist presence in several communities of the British Columbia interior. The presence and example of non-whites like the Wings may have been a critical factor in softening public opinion and mitigating public policy toward non-citizen residents, but hard times continued to play on racist sentiments.

With the completion of the railway, many Chinese, Japanese and East Indians moved from railroad construction to farming. In the early 1920s market gardening made a substantial contribution to the Kamloops economy. At one point, three canneries in Kamloops were shipping tomatoes, beans and pumpkins to other parts of the country. "White only" hiring policies were briefly dropped due to a labour shortage, but prejudice was strongly felt by immigrant workers. The Broder Canning Company, which commenced production in 1926, failed largely due to white workers refusing to cooperate with a Chinese foreman. A fight between two men in the Kamloops Cannery was falsely reported by the *Kamloops Sentinel* as a war between the Chinese and Hindus. Coming into the 1930s, the Kamloops and Carlin Canneries once again introduced "white only" hiring policies.

The market gardens of Kamloops could not complete with the lush fields of the Fraser Valley from which the railway offered regular delivery of fresh and processed produce to the British Columbia interior. The local market gardens and canneries gradually declined. With no work and little opportunity, the immigrant working men moved on. What had once been a thriving Chinatown gradually disappeared. It had twice been rebuilt following major fires in 1892 and 1893. It had survived demolition in 1913 when the railroad, which had run down the middle of the main street, was moved closer to the South Thompson River, but it would not survive The Great Depression. By the 1940s most Chinese had moved away. For the Wings, who were established in the business community and lived outside the confines of Chinatown, there was little change.

"We lived basically for work," explained Peter. *"Everything we did and everything everybody else did in [our] particular line of business [was done] in the same way. We didn't think we were any different from anybody else."*

At the end of 1934 the Wings had returned from Hong Kong in the midst of hard times for Kamloops. Soup kitchens were serving up to 460 men per day. More men arrived daily, riding the rails in search of work. When the province established work camps throughout British Columbia, 750 men registered in Kamloops. Asians were excluded. Peter felt that prejudice against Asians was much more open and public in Canada than the racial bias experienced by blacks in the United States during the same period. "White Only" hiring in business was one thing. Exclusion from government aid programs was another. Neither was justifiable.

After the invasion of Manchuria in 1931, public opinion toward the Chinese in British Columbia had begun to soften. As the war in China progressed and British interests became threatened, China and the Chinese were seen as allies and friends. By 1935 the communities of British Columbia accepted responsibility to assist their Chinese populations, but with much lower benefits than those offered to whites.

Significantly, the local Chinese population was more generous in its support of the country than other groups within Kamloops. In 1936, Kamloops' Chinese donated a rail car full of produce to drought-stricken Saskatchewan – their commitment to the larger community of Canada during the "Dirty Thirties." Local Chinese support of the Kamloops Royal Inland Hospital amounted to ten tons of produce annually. Second-generation Chinese in Canada were concerned for their cousins in China, but saw themselves first as Canadians, even though the rest of the country did not.

In this atmosphere, Eng continued developing the family business. He kept emphasizing to his children, *"Don't get anything until you can pay for it!"* Peter's view of credit cards and the exorbitant interest charges that accompany them probably came from the family experience of the 1930s.

"All this advertising... no payments for a year or no interest. Those are what I call U.S. influence. It was developed in the United States, enlarged and then stretched over to this side. They keep complaining about the credit card interest. You never have to pay interest if you pay your credit card account at the right time. That's a penalty. That's the way it should be."

With the social atmosphere seemingly stacked against him, Eng found himself in somewhat of a dilemma. His family was too Chinese to be accepted in a white British society and had found itself too Canadian to blend into the Chinese culture of Hong Kong. As Chinese, the Wings were denied voting rights in Provincial and Municipal elections and therefore had no say in governmental decisions that directly affected their family. However, there was no law barring them from the civic associations and service clubs that keep a town functioning. The Wings could not participate in the decision-making, but as an upstanding family, they could affect the decision makers. The timing could not have been better.

The Kamloops Board of Trade (later to become the Chamber of Commerce) was recruiting younger members to the Board of Trade, which had become an "old boys" club. Ross Dagleish, an active board member, asked Peter if he would join. Dagleish saw the Wings as good progressive businessmen with a strong commitment to the community. He also understood that as non-citizens they had little influence in business or community concerns. By this time Eng had served Kamloops for over thirty years. Some board members had known Peter from the time he was born. They had seen him grow up, serve tables, drive the family delivery truck and run the family business. According to Peter, half or more of the Board were members of the United Church. They had sat next to the Wings in worship and listened as Peter sang in the church choir. The Wings were respected and thought of as valued

citizens, not as alien Chinese. In a sense, beginning with the Board of
Trade, community leaders "allowed" the Wings admission to the community. Peter himself commented, "*I was only allowed to do what society
would let me do.*"

Membership on the Board of Trade gave the Wings a way to express
their needs and the needs of the local Chinese community. For the
first time they had not only a presence, but also a voice in shaping
Kamloops as it is known today.

"*At that time the Chinese people weren't considered 'people' legally, but
partially socially [sic],*" said Peter. "*The people could see that we were doing
a good business and they knew that we didn't have any say [in city affairs].
He [Dagliesh] asked me to join. I was only twenty years old at the time and
there was hardly anybody under fifty in the Board of Trade.*

"*In self-defence, my father decided I should join. That's the only way we
could have a say in the business affairs of the city. We could legally buy and
sell property and that's about it. Only a handful of the members were active,
so [there was] ample opportunity [to serve].*"

Board of Trade members at that time were a close-knit group with
personal ties in church, in business and in the community at large. They
were intimately in touch with the needs of the city. The approximately
forty members gave positive approval for Peter's membership. Since
only about a dozen members were fully active, Peter found himself
immediately appointed to their working committees. Soon he took
part in almost every project the Board sponsored.

This also placed Peter in position to interpret for local Chinese
residents involved in business and court proceedings. Members of
the Board of Trade came to greatly respect and trust the young Asian.
Almost 20 years later, in 1953, Peter would be elected Vice President
of the Board. Eventually, these many years of public service opened
the door to Peter's civic service in City Hall. Time, testing and con-
sistency gave him a reputation as an active worker and reliable leader
that endured for over 60 years. When Peter was interviewed in 1999, he
was one of the oldest continuous members of the Kamloops Chamber

of Commerce (originally the Board of Trade), carrying an honorary lifetime membership.

Meanwhile, the C.C.F. party (the Co-operative Commonwealth Federation) had picked up the Chinese cause for citizenship and equal opportunity at the provincial level. The C.C.F. had been founded in 1932 in Calgary, Alberta as a political coalition of progressives, socialists and labour. Their purpose was to bring relief to those suffering the effects of the Great Depression. Liberals in the election of 1935 charged that a vote for the C.C.F. was a vote for Asian enfranchisement, a move that played on the distressing economic woes of the average Canadian and on his residual fear of the "Yellow Peril." Sadly, the time of the "Chinese Canadian" was not yet to be. After World War II the C.C.F. fell victim to the Cold War with accusations of being associated with communism and the party gradually declined. In an effort to revive democratic socialism, the remnant of the C.C.F. would eventually join forces with the Canadian Labour Congress in 1961 to form the New Democratic Party.

Entering into the 1940s Chinese farmers were gradually gaining control of wholesale market gardening in southern British Columbia. The co-operative marketing strategy of the Asians was seen as a way to gain at least some control of pricing. It didn't resonate well with white farmers, but for the Chinese farmers it was a matter of economic survival.

Two factors kept the Wings in a good financial position throughout the Depression. First, was the Chinese tradition that extended families share household space, income and expense. Second, was The Cut Rate Self-Serve Grocery. A grocery store that deals with commodities and consumables could hardly fail. No matter how harsh the economy, people have to eat. What was a troubled economy for some was economic opportunity for others. In 1936, the Freemont block of downtown Kamloops was placed on the market and Eng had money to invest. Due to the financial realities of the time, the property came at a good price.

John Freemont Smith, who owned the property, is worthy of mention. He was a pioneer in the Kamloops community who established a successful bakery in 1888. The same year, together with members of the Kamloops Indian Band, now known as the Tk'emlúps Band, and Chief Petit Louis (Hli Kleh Kan), Smith organised a prospecting expedition into the Cariboo Mountains.

A gold rush had transpired in the region between 1860 and 1863. Visitors to the British Columbia interior will find a trip to historic Barkerville, now a "living history" community in the Cariboo region, a worthwhile visit. The site includes the restoration of one of Canada's oldest Chinatowns and confirms the contribution of Chinese prospectors in opening up the British Columbia interior. The Chinese population in Barkerville was large enough to maintain its own school. Today the opportunity to see people living as they did in the 1860s and to pan your own gold is quite exciting.

Active mining in the area ended in the 1930s. Smith's group had set out to explore large mica deposits in the provincial interior. In Freemont Smith's case the prospecting did not pay.

Smith later became Secretary of the Board of Trade and was a tireless promoter of community business. He founded the Kamloops Agricultural Association and Farmer's Institutes and served as Indian Agent from 1912 to 1923. John Freemont Smith made the claim of being the first "white" man up the North Thompson River. Ironically, Smith was a "black" Jamaican. He led the way for minority leaders like Peter Wing to take their rightful place in the community. Smith was retired by the time Peter entered the Board of Trade, but he was still well-known in Kamloops.

The Depression, the family business and the Board of Trade were not enough for Peter's inexhaustible supply of energy. During the 30s he took violin lessons, joined the Royal Canadian Legion Junior Symphony, played the organ for the Chinese Mission and sang in the United Church Choir. It seems that his every interest and talent eventually expressed itself in some form of public service or community involvement: his business experience – the Board of Trade;

his interest in automobiles and mechanics – the British Columbia Auto Association; his orchard experience – the B.C. Fruit Growers Association; his music – the Junior Symphony and United Church Choir. For Peter, every talent learned was a talent to be shared. Perhaps his greatest talent was the sharing itself, which he expressed in loyal support and execution of projects others had already begun.

Eng Wing   Peter Wing

Father and son combining a winning combination of vision, loyalty and service in building a future for their family and acceptance of Chinese Canadians by the larger community.
(photos – Kamloops Museum & Archives #5261, #6877)

Chapter 6

THE WAR AT HOME

*Don't waste good iron for nails, or good
men for soldiers. (Chinese Proverb)*

While Peter was establishing himself in the Board of Trade and learning the art of getting things done in the public service, Britain declared war on Germany in early September, 1939. As the Commonwealth countries marshalled their support, countries like Canada, with its diverse ethnic mosaic, faced unique challenges. Chinese men, including Peter, who was Canadian born, were still denied the rights and privileges of citizenship. Yet, they were included in the general military conscription introduced towards the end of the war and Peter, along with others, responded to the call.

"Dr. Archibald, known as "Castor Oil Slim" because of his favourite general prescription, was one of our family physicians," recalled Peter. *"I took my draft notice to him for the medical. He said, 'You didn't need to come. I could have filled the medical in and sent it for you. With your eyes the way they are and after that session in the hospital, I can't pass you.' So I*

*became co-chairman of the air raid precautions for the city. In a way I was
relieved because I was to all intents and purposes head of the family."*

Peter pointed to the Victory loans and War Savings Certificates as
examples of the commitment of resident Chinese to the allied cause. In
1944, the Kamloops Chinese subscribed an average of $202 per person,
a record for the country.

"We all worked really hard raising funds for the war," he said.

Two of Kim's brothers joined the Canadian army: George saw
action in Europe where he was wounded and received the Medal of
France and Jim was still in active training as the war ended. Kim's
brother-in-law, Wilson Lee, served in Canada and later in Britain as a
medical officer.

The wartime experience of Kim's cousin, Gin Lew, provides insight
into how North American Chinese viewed themselves. Gin had emi-
grated to the United States where he was drafted into the U.S. Army.
His basic training took place in the American south where segregation
still reigned. Not being "black" in his own eyes, he didn't realise he was
considered a "coloured" person until entering a restaurant that posted
a sign, "WE DON'T SERVE COLOURED PEOPLE." The manager
refused to serve him and asked Gin to leave. He soon returned with
two large very black MPs. A terrified manager was told, "You are not
serving us as people. You are serving the United States uniform." The
sign was quickly removed and according to Gin, the service was great!

Unable to enlist and serving on the home front wherever he could,
Peter's attention turned to an important family crisis. In 1940 his
brother, Jim, broke a leg in a bicycle accident. The attending doctor left
on vacation without giving proper instructions for Jim's convalescence
and gangrene set into the limb. Peter spent much of the next two years
transporting Jim between Kamloops and Vancouver in a desperate
attempt to save his leg. Eventually the leg was amputated.

Meanwhile, with the occupation of China by Japan, sympathy was
growing for the Chinese in general. The likeable "Charlie Chan" with
his many numbered sons replaced the evil "Fu Manchu" in Hollywood.
Interestingly, the *Charlie Chan* series did not reach popularity with the

predominately white audience until the Korean actor, E.L. Park, was replaced by a white Swedish actor, Warner Oland. Critics of the series felt it reinforced the biased stereotype that North American Chinese were bound by tradition, incapable of proper English and subservient to authority. Proponents of the series, which produced over four dozen movies and ran for more than two decades, pointed to Charlie Chan as an example of Asian intelligence, fearlessness, generosity and integrity.

It must be noted that concern for mainland China by North American Chinese, like the Wings and Kwongs, was not that of exiled or displaced people for their homeland. Even while maintaining certain cultural traditions and language, these families stayed in Canada as immigrant settlers. China was to the Canadian Chinese what Europe was to Canadian Europeans. The main difference between Asian and European immigrants was citizenship. The fact that Canada, apart from its First Nations people, is an immigrant country seems to have been overlooked. The Canadian Chinese commitment to the country, its laws and its future was simply not recognised, at least not in a way that counted.

With Japan being perceived as an "aggressor nation" and the Japanese in North America being a very visible minority, conditions became extremely difficult for the Japanese living in both Canada and the United States. The bombing of Pearl Harbor was followed six months later with the shelling of the Estevan Point lighthouse on the west coast of Vancouver Island and the bombing of Dutch Harbor, a small American naval base in the Aleutian Islands of Alaska. Fear of a west coast invasion by Japan fuelled a powerful movement for the internment of all Japanese immigrants in western Canada.

In 1942, the Canadian Legion passed a resolution that all Japanese be placed under guard. Kamloops City Council supported the motion. The Kamloops Board of Trade and Liberal Association opposed any movement of Japanese from the coast to the British Columbia interior. The general feeling was internment, yes, but not in their neighborhood.

In spite of the protest by interior communities, an internment camp housing 600 people was built about 200 kilometres north of Kamloops near Blue River. This shameful displacement of Canadian immigrants was not enforced on those Japanese already living in central British Columbia, but Kamloops City Council members requested that the BC Security Commission declare their community a restricted zone because of its ammunition dumps and railways. In 1943, one area was restricted and George Oishi, a Japanese orchardist, was forced to leave his farm.

"[George] had to move because there was an ammo dump adjoining his orchard," said Peter. *"He had leased a couple acres for the ammo dump to have a service garage and a pumping station. His friends in the fruit business suggested that I could take over and he would come out better than he would with whatever the government would have given him. He would have been lucky if he got $5,000. We arrived at a value and paid $21,000 for a 35-acre orchard, the equipment and house. I think he must have foreseen the [move], because in the meantime he bought property in [the] Powers Addition. Right after we bought from him he started a market there. He ran that for about 10 years."*

The Wings referred to these events as a *"sad time."* They had not maintained ties with China and considered themselves Canadian even though the country did not. They saw their Japanese neighbours in the same light. The historical record shows there was never any trouble with the Japanese in the Kamloops region. After 1944, with no major invasion of Canada's West Coast and no sabotage within the country, fear of Japanese immigrants began to abate. Racial bigotry of the time greatly eclipsed any actual risk.

During the 1940s Peter became more and more involved with community organisations. The war effort overseas had left a leadership vacuum on the home front. Part of Peter Wing's success in Kamloops was simply a matching of the right man to the right time. He was already established in the Chamber of Commerce (formerly the Board of Trade) when the Junior Chamber of Commerce was founded, so he chose to maintain his membership as it was. He did, however, give support to the JCs by providing free office space and personally participating in many of their community projects.

The Junior Chamber of Commerce introduced Peter to the wiles of public opinion. The group had taken on the project of cleaning up an old cemetery located west of the present Columbo Hall on Lorne Street. The care of the cemetery had been neglected for many years and the grounds were in a state of weeds and disarray.

"It was a mess! The headstones had been knocked over... in those days they had big headstones," Peter remembered. "It was very weedy and the Junior Chamber of Commerce decided they wanted to clean it up. They called me... I had the farm then, so I had the equipment to do it. I went down, had a couple work parties and cleaned it up... moved the headstones into one corner. You should have heard some of the letters to the editor. We were 'desecrating' the cemetery. Most people didn't even know it was there. One person I knew quite well had ancestors in the cemetery. He said, 'That's the best thing you could have done.' Spiritually and from a religious point of view, as long as the memory is there, the remains don't mean that much to me. Memory, not remains, is what is important. The remains go back to dust. That's part of our funeral service."

In return for his support and participation, the Junior Chamber of Commerce later appointed Peter as "Governor #38" within the local chapter.

In 1941, Peter joined a service club that succinctly defined his philosophy of life, Rotary International. Rotary, North America's oldest service club, was founded in 1905 by Paul Harris in Chicago, Illinois. In 1911, a Canadian chapter opened in Winnipeg, Manitoba. Eleven years later, in 1922, Dr. R.W. Irving introduced Rotary to Kamloops. That same year the club officially became "Rotary International." The club supports many social and community welfare projects and is a leader in scholarship programs promoting foreign exchange students and foreign study. Rotary's Four-Way Test of the things we think, say and do reflected Peter Wing's personal philosophy very well:

1. Is it the TRUTH?
2. Is it FAIR to all concerned?
3. Will it build GOODWILL and BETTER FRIENDSHIPS?
4. Will it be BENEFICIAL to all concerned?

"That's what I've tried to live by," Peter said. *"As luck would have it, the year that I joined was the year that the four-way test was established, 1942.*

"Rotary at that time had what we called the 'Spokes Club.' We would meet once a month at somebody's home and the chairman would give somebody a subject to talk on. It made good speakers of many of us. For my own part, that's what got me started. I had no academic training, so it worked out very well."

Rotary led to many contacts and much travel for Peter and Kim. Peter recalled a Rotary conference they attended in Dallas, Texas. They sat behind some Alabaman delegates who were upset that racial clauses had been removed from the original Rotary constitution.

"This fellow turned around and of course, he couldn't see that I was a different ethnic origin, and he says, 'It wasn't the coloured people who were against it. It was the niggers!' It was said as if 'niggers' were a type of animal. Animals would never treat each other as do people."

The Wings understood prejudice in a very personal way and worked hard to bring down the racial divisions between people.

Kim Wing, always supportive of Peter, was making her own quiet contribution in the community. Her membership in Soroptimist International complemented Peter's involvement in Rotary. The Soroptimists are a global movement of business and professional women dedicated to the empowerment of women. By coincidence, Kim was writing a Soroptimist in Sao Paulo, Brazil. They met in person at a World Rotary Conference in Sao Paulo. Her sister Soroptimist was cousin to the conference host.

Peter took great pride in the student exchange program sponsored by the Kamloops chapter of Rotary. Each year three exchanges are made in the spirit of promoting good will and understanding between communities of different nations. Until their later years, Peter and Kim had a personal tradition of hosting an evening meal in their home for visiting students.

In the '40s, the Wings also joined the Canadian Council of Christians and Jews and the Canadian Mosaic Club. The latter service club advances appreciation for the differing Canadian cultures, which Peter described as being *"like a succulent meal, each part adding its own variety and attractiveness."* To him it would be a shame to simply *"mince the whole and blend its distinctions."* He was very direct in stating, *"We in Canada are a mosaic of many cultures and we don't want to become a stew like the United States."*

Chapter 7

A NEST OF THEIR OWN

When wings are grown, birds and children fly away. (Chinese Proverb)

Purchase of the Oishi property in 1943 began a new chapter for Peter and Kim. The Orchard, 35 acres on the site of the present Orchard Park Subdivision, was their first real home as a couple. For more than ten years they had managed the Wing household for Eng and Lin. Peter had never worked outside the family business. The farm was a new and exciting adventure.

Being a hands-on person and loving mechanical things, farming offered Peter a little of everything. Three tractors were used in the operation. Over the next 15 years not one ever saw a commercial shop for maintenance or repairs. The mechanical and business aspects of farming were second nature, but horticulture was another story. Other orchardists, especially the McGillivrays, taught him the basic operation of farming. Time and experience taught the rest.

"*We were never on our own until we bought the orchard,*" said Peter.
"*I hardly knew an apple tree from a fir tree, but the people that encouraged me to buy the place were very good. They never let me [make any foolish mistakes].*

"*We bought the orchard in the fall of '43. In the spring of '44 there was a fruit grower's association meeting in Vernon. They encouraged me to go and I was put on the board of the association immediately.*"

Although a rookie, Peter was appointed as Director for the Kamloops district. He held the position until the sale of the orchard in 1957. It was an interesting time for BC fruit growers. British Columbia Fruit Processors Limited was established in Kelowna. Its purpose was to study the use of excess and low-grade fruit which otherwise would be discarded. The company's first product was 100 percent pure apple juice. Other products followed. In 1959 the company took on a new name and a new look, Sun-Rype Products Ltd.

Many of Kim's fondest memories went back to the farm, which was their first real home as a couple.

Kim: "*There was hardly a weekend in the summer when we didn't have fifteen or twenty at the table. The nieces and nephews were just like our own. [They had] a lot of fun. There were tractors and ditches and everything. I remember the day when David, [Peter's youngest brother by about twenty years] stuck his feet down the hole in the ditch. Out comes a muskrat!*"

Peter: "*We raised chickens for food, even tried raising rabbits. We had a dog because of wild animals, [just like the] restaurant always had a cat.*"

The farm offered privacy and freedom that had been unknown in the household of Peter's parents.

Kim: "*Every winter we took a trip, usually into southern California, because in the winter months you didn't have that much to do operating an orchard. So we did a little bit of traveling. We were instigators of a couples' club in our church. We would meet in each other's homes or at the church. That's the kind of thing we enjoyed very much.*"

The orchard put to use Peter's skills as mechanic, bookkeeper, manager and businessman. Many years later he could still recite and compare fruit production rates of Kamloops, the Okanagan and

Eastern Washington. Winters were off times, but spring and summer was busy. Peter soon added to his work dossier the position of foreman.

"*Part-time labour, like pruning and that sort of thing, depended on the natives across the river,*" said Peter. "*I [also] had the advantage of the soldiers that were working in the ammo dump. They were great, especially the French Canadians. They helped us quite a lot. That worked out very well.*"

In addition to farming Peter continued his contribution to family business ventures. In 1947, Eng began construction of the Wing Building, a major structure in downtown Kamloops at the corner of 3rd Avenue and Victoria Street. Peter personally installed about half the wiring in the building. Now 68 years later (2016), the Kipp-Mallery Pharmacy, one of the original tenants, still occupies space in the building.

The farm provided an oasis of predictability during the social and political changes of the early postwar years. In 1946, labour unions, the C.C.F. party and Canadian veterans' organisations lobbied hard for Chinese enfranchisement. Any man good enough to work on the manufacturing line and brave enough to fight for the country was man enough to share the vote. Finally, in 1947, the day of the Chinese Canadian arrived. Citizenship was approved for *resident* Chinese immigrants. *Wives and unmarried children* could now join their husbands and fathers in Canada. This was a progressive step, but still very restrictive compared to immigration laws applied to Europeans. It is hard to believe, but only an estimated 15 Chinese had been admitted to Canada as immigrants between 1924 and 1947.

Peter: "*The first thing my father did was to get his citizenship papers. At long last we were able to do something. I finally felt that I was a part of the country. I'm proud of the fact that I've been able to be a part of this country and that I was accepted as well as I was.*"

Kim: "*There wasn't too much celebrating. All along we had had a good life.*"

The Wings had always considered Canada as their home. They had dutifully attended the July 1st Canada Day celebrations year after year and had faithfully promoted the local community where they lived and worked. Citizenship gave them security and permanence within Canada. The vote allowed them a voice in the nation's business.

Peter was 34 years old when he cast his first ballot as a registered voter in 1948.

"The only time I didn't vote Liberal was when Davey Fulton, [a Conservative], got in," said Peter.

Fulton was two years younger than Peter and had often called on him for motorcycle repairs. Fulton wasn't even home when nominated and elected, but his family was well-known. His older brother, Jack, was a local hero because of his service in World War II. Jack had commanded Squadron 419 of the Royal Canadian Air Force and had quite a reputation for his commitment to the welfare of his men. The story was well-known of an incident in which a crippled aircraft of his squadron was unable to make the return trip from a mission over Europe. Shortly after an emergency landing in a small remote British airstrip, the bomber crew was astonished to see Commander Fulton driving in to account for all his men. Later, when Fulton was killed in action, the squadron took his nickname, "Moose." With much effort on the part of his men, the squadron eventually received official recognition as No. 419 Moose Squadron, RCAF. If you fly into Kamloops today you will land at the Kamloops airport, "Fulton Field."

We have to wonder why Peter turned to the Liberal Party and not the C.C.F. (now the New Democratic Party). The C.C.F. was the only political party that strongly lobbied for Chinese citizenship, which the Liberal party actively opposed. Yet, Peter chose the party representing a "middle path" between socialism and conservatism, a party that to him seemed best suited to the common good and needs of the majority.

The historical roots of the Liberal party in Kamloops may have influenced the Wing position. Kamloops has a long tradition of Liberal Senators in Parliament, including Senator Hewitt Bostock (1904), Sydney John Smith (1957) and Leonard Marchand (1984). The Wings knew all three. Peter's involvement with the Liberals eventually led to an honorary chairmanship of the Liberal Association in Kamloops, which he held until his death.

Citizenship opened many doors for Chinese Canadians. Jim Kwong, Kim's brother, graduated from the University of British Columbia in the early 1950s with his Bachelor of Commerce degree and the desire to be a chartered accountant. Previously the profession had been closed to the Chinese. French and Barrow Chartered Accountants of Kamloops led the Association of Chartered Accountants by accepting Jim as an articled student. When he completed his articles and passed the examinations, Jim Kwong became the first chartered accountant of Chinese ancestry in Canada.

From the time of his rheumatic fever as a boy, Peter had never been laid up. In 1954, this changed when he went for major back surgery. At the same time, the fruit industry in the Kamloops area was rapidly becoming marginal. The time had come for a change in career. The Kamloops' orchards and canneries were vanishing due to simple economics. Interior British Columbian soil and climate could not produce the same tonnage as its southern neighbours.

In 1957, a contractor made Peter an offer for the orchard property.

"By the time I got this offer to sell the place for a subdivision," said Peter, *"it had become pretty marginal as far as income was concerned. I sold the orchard and built the apartment building. [The orchard] only paid for half of it, but I was able to build it so that I had it paid off in about five years."*

One of the early tenants of the Wing Apartments was Len Marchand, who was to become Canada's first elected Aboriginal Minister of Parliament and later, Senate appointee. Peter recalled the young, newly married Len moving into a suite of the apartments in the 1960s and claims indirect credit for Len's marriage to Donna Parr. The story goes that Len, who was working as a technician at the Department of Agriculture station just outside of Kamloops, had a classmate named Sandy McCurrach. Sandy rented an apartment from the Wings that was next door to two young nurses, Donna Parr and Barbara Shea. One evening while Len was visiting Sandy, smoke alerted them to a fire next door. Len and Sandy ran over to help. Peter came from downstairs to see who was *"burning down the building."* The smoke was coming from a burnt stew. According to Peter, Len met Donna in the process. They eventually married and began their life together in the Wing building. It is doubtful that Len married Donna for her cooking skills, but to be fair, Len Marchand does not mention this incident in his autobiography and Donna would not confirm it when interviewed.

Television was just coming out when the Wings moved from the farm.

"The first TV I had was when my brother went to the British Columbia School of Technology," recalled Peter. *"During his time there he built a TV set. That's the first TV set we ever had. It was just set up on a box. We had that for quite a while."*

Like the early radios, early television posed some reception challenges. It's not hard to imagine Peter on the roof positioning the antenna with its multiple prongs and calling to Kim, "Is that better? How about this?" There would be no scanning the airwaves with TV. Reception was limited to local CFCR-TV (later to become CFJC).

Peter was not one to stay at home watching television and seems to have inherited his father's entrepreneurial spirit. He had served in the restaurant, managed the grocery, mastered the farm, built the apartments and was still looking for something more. So he signed on with J.W. Hall, of Hall & Pruden Real Estate, as a real estate and insurance salesman. Within two years he bought the business, renaming it "Peter Wing Real Estate."

"I got my real estate sales license in 1957 and in 1959, the agent's license. I bought the real estate firm at that time. The biggest deal I made was the sale of the Bostock Ranch. (The Monte Creek or Duck's Ranch was originally homesteaded in the 1850s by a Mexican known as "Monte" and purchased by Hewitt Bostock in 1888.) That was an historic ranch in Kamloops. Bostock was the first senator from Kamloops. By the time the ranch was up for sale there were just two sisters left of the family and they listed it with me. The fellow I had for a salesman was very close to them, so between us we had a pretty good rapport. I hired a helicopter to take a prospect around the place. One of the agencies associated with us sold it.

"*In 1960 I went into politics and that kind of slowed down the business. You can't be a member of council and operate a real estate business. I had a couple of good salesmen, [but] we didn't go out for sales aggressively because that would have been a conflict of interest. We didn't do badly; we've always lived quite comfortably.*

"*Grocer, farmer, realtor, that's what I'm generally known as,*" concluded Peter.

Income from the apartment building along with what little commission Peter received from the real estate firm were important sources of income during his later years in City Hall. In those years the mayor and aldermen at City Hall received very small stipends and paid many of their work-related expenses out of pocket. They served as "civic servants" in the true sense of the term.

Chapter 8

CITY HALL

*Stout men, not stout walls, make the
stout city. (Chinese Proverb)*

At the end of the 1950s, elected city officials were largely self-support-ing, receiving only a modest stipend for their service. When Peter sat as alderman in 1960, his annual stipend was $1,200 per year. In 1971, when he sat as mayor, he received $6,600. Travel on behalf of the community was paid for out of pocket. Public service required financial sacrifice. Between the Wing apartments and his real estate business, Peter was in a good financial position to serve the community on a full-time basis. In the fall of 1959, friends in the Chamber of Commerce urged him to run for City Council and he was ready for the challenge.

In the City Council meeting of January, 1960, Peter Wing took his seat as a city alderman. Having been active in the Chamber of Commerce for close to 30 years and having rendered service in the Fruit Growers Association, the Canadian Mosaic, the United Church and other organisations, he was not looked upon as Chinese, but rather as Canadian. His peers saw him as a good citizen and a good community servant. Apart from his early school days he was not looked upon as an outsider. Peter's career as a public servant was filled with various memberships, projects and trips.

Although aldermen sat for two years, elections were held in December of each year with half the council of six aldermen taking office on alternate years. This ensured a continuity of experienced members in Council. In 1961, Peter's second year as alderman, J.E. Fitzwater was elected for his fifth consecutive term as Mayor, the longest continuous term in that Kamloops office to-date. At that time, City Hall operated through Council Committees and a City Clerk. Peter served the system well through three terms as an alderman. He loved the challenges of running a city and being the only alderman with real estate experience he had valuable experience to offer the Council. The MacIntosh subdivision had just opened to the market and Mayor Fitzwater assigned Peter to recommend pricing for the new building lots. Peter's recommendations were accepted and the lots readily sold. One of the buyers he remembers was Phil Gaglardi, M.L.A. and Minister of Highways. Gaglardi would later serve as Kamloops Mayor in 1989.

As an alderman Peter joined other members of Council at a meeting of the Okanagan Valley Municipal Association (O.V.M.A.). This association of municipalities worked together to effectively voice common community concerns and initiatives. With his previous participation in the British Columbia Fruit Growers' Association, Peter already knew many of the delegates. In time he was elected as a Director of the O.V.M.A. and later became President of the association. Because the communities of Kamloops, Salmon Arm and Revelstoke were also members of the association, but not located within the Okanagan Valley, Peter proposed a new name for the organization, the Okanagan-Mainline Municipal Association (O.M.M.A.). Members accepted the name and the association is still in operation. 1963 saw Peter's appointment as a delegate representing the O.M.M.A. at the 26th annual conference of the Canadian Federation of Mayors and Municipalities, now known as the Federation of Canadian Municipalities.

Those were busy but rewarding years. Aldermen and Mayors from across Canada were working on mutual problems and policies. The conferences and meetings were valuable preparation for Peter's later tenure as Mayor of Kamloops. Topics discussed included inter-municipal cooperation in urban development and the administrative structure of municipal governments. Peter was elected president of the Union of British Columbia Municipalities, which was similar to the national association. Following his chairmanship, he continued as a Director until he retired.

In the early 1960s numerous charities regularly canvassed the different neighbourhoods in Kamloops. Peter had personally knocked on virtually every door in Kamloops while helping various causes. He shared the chairmanship of the Red Shield, the Salvation Army's major fundraiser, for four years. It seems that his "hands-on" approach carried into his public service just as it had in his private life.

"Before the United Way was instituted, we had regular canvasses of the town for different [causes]... Salvation Army, Red Cross and so on. It got to a point where some of us were out every other week," said Peter.

The idea of the United Way, in which one general collection is divided proportionately between the major charities, came to Kamloops while Peter was an alderman. Having personally experienced the effort required of different institutions to raise funds, he endorsed and promoted the United Way as a means of cooperative support for suitable community charities.

With all his energy, networking and experience, it is not surprising that Peter was asked to run for Mayor. His campaign advertisement in the December 9, 1965 *Kamloops Daily Sentinel* read, "I am prepared to give the time and pledge myself to continue to work in the interests of all the people in Kamloops." Bold type read, "THE MAN WITH YOU IN MIND."

Following the vote, the December 13th edition of the *Kamloops Daily Sentinel* stated, "Peter Wing, who staged a big upset in the Kamloops mayoralty race, also established two firsts for the city in civic elections. He is the first native-born son of the city to become mayor and is also believed to be the first Canadian of Chinese ancestry to become mayor of a Canadian city."

In fact, he was the first person of Chinese ancestry to become mayor anywhere in North America. In the three-way race for mayor, Peter Wing won with 39 percent of the vote. Gardner Boultbee took 33 percent and the incumbent, Mayor Cyril Day, received 28 percent. "His Worship Peter Wing" took mayoral office in January of 1966. Regarding public titles, Peter wryly commented, *"In the United States they refer to their mayors as 'honorable,' whereas in the British tradition we in Canada refer to them as 'Your Worship.' The Americans honour their mayors; we worship ours."*

Much to Peter's credit, he never pursued a personal agenda leading to office or prestige. He simply responded to the needs of the community and fulfilled those which were within his reach. In his leadership role he pursued the principle of cooperation in seeking the common good rather than competition in seeking narrow regional interests. Whatever conflicts he faced with other members of various boards and councils he chose not to relate when interviewed. He would rather discuss overall accomplishments and let bygones be bygones. It was important to him that there be no offence to either his critics or their families. This particular attitude explains why in his service as Mayor there was rarely any conflict within City Council. Peter conducted city business much as his own father had conducted the family business. He saw himself as a team leader and not as "the boss."

"When I was in Council I had no problems at all. It just felt natural to get in the Chair and then do things."

A family medical emergency threatened to end Peter's first term within days of taking office. Kim Wing was diagnosed with cervical cancer, which needed immediate attention.

Peter: *"Part of the problem was that we had so many health professionals in our family that we were 'doctored' to death. Three of [Kim's] sisters*

are nurses and I have a sister that's a nurse and one of [Kim's] sister's hus-
bands is a doctor. So we had lots of advice."

Kim: *"It was Dr. Smiley who found what I had and wanted me to have*
the operation here, but my sister wouldn't hear of it [and] made other
arrangements. Smiley was raising Cain. It gets you in a spot where you don't
know what to do. I got the surgery in Vancouver because we were closer to
family there."

Peter: *"We pretty well accepted things as they came, but it was a shock*
at first. Except for broken bones that was the first major medical problem
we ever had."

Kim recovered quickly and the couple took the opportunity to get
away while attending an international conference entitled, "Emergency
Measures Organization." The conference explored the operation of
local governments during major disasters, a timely subject at that point
in the Cold War. That year the conference was conducted in Arnprior,
Ontario. Peter recalled that one of the instructors, an Italian, opened
a meeting with, "I must remember to speak English today." When
Peter spoke, he spoke in Cantonese the equivalent of, "Good morning,
ladies and gentlemen." He then explained that though none in the class
understood his greeting, ten percent of the Vancouver population
would have understood perfectly.

Since Arnprior is close to Ottawa, the Wings took time to visit the
nation's capital. Syd Smith, a resident of Kamloops and the original
owner of Smith Chevrolet Cadillac Ltd., was then sitting as Speaker
of the Senate. He introduced the Wings to many members of both
Houses. Peter was becoming a respected figure in municipal, provincial and now federal circles in Canada. He enjoyed the tour and joked,
"I really got a royal tour and I didn't even buy a car from him."

When they returned to Kamloops, the time had come for Peter
to apply himself to the management of city government. At that time,
Kamloops and North Kamloops were two separate municipalities.
Talks of amalgamation had begun in 1964. At a city council meeting
February 23, 1965, Peter, as an Alderman, had stated, *"Amalgamation*
of our two communities could be of greater immediate advantage to North

Kamloops than to the City of Kamloops, but would, in an overall picture, benefit both communities." Former North Kamloops mayor, Don Ellsay, strongly opposed the move and took the news media to task, calling them "promoters, judge, jury, pro-amalgamation and little tin gods" in the city council meeting of October 25th, 1965. Peter later recalled that Ellsay *"was always negative, no matter how good a thing was. He was always a parochial person."*

In June of 1966, just a little over five months into Peter's first term as mayor, the proposed union of the two municipalities was put to a referendum. Amalgamation won with more than 75 percent of the vote. This was the second incorporation of two communities in Canadian history. The first was the amalgamation of the Ontario cities of Fort William and Port Arthur as Thunder Bay. The formal ceremony uniting Kamloops and North Kamloops occurred November 3, 1967, Canada's Centennial year. The two councils, with their mayors, Chilton and Wing, acted jointly until the December elections.

In 1967, Mayor Wing could seemingly do no wrong. That year, Peter acted as chairman for the Centennial celebrations and actually played the organ for "O Canada" during the festivities. He also chaired the regional citizenship ceremonies. When the Mayor's seat came up for election at the end of the year Mayor Wing was so popular that he was returned to office by acclamation. His reputation was such that there was talk in Revelstoke about asking him to serve as mayor there at the same time. There is really no great event or achievement that Peter's popularity can be credited to. He was simply a loyal, dedicated civil servant who did his job very well.

"I got into everything I've done because people thought I could do the job and encouraged me to do it. I've never gone into a position where I would say, 'Oh, that position is open. I'm going to take it.' Most of us that do things don't realize we are doing anything special when we are doing it," Peter explained.

Peter was living evidence of the proverb, "Do you see a man who excels in his work? He will stand before kings; He will not stand before unknown men" (Proverbs 22:29).

The same year, Peter attended a meeting of the International Union of Local Authorities (IULA) in Bangkok, Thailand along with municipal officials from most of the free world. The IULA began in Holland in 1913 with the objective of supporting local self-government of cities and municipalities. Training institutions, corporations and individuals are brought together to exchange ideas, information and expertise. The cross-cultural contact contributes to the betterment of all.

Kamloops City Council had authorised the trip and paid the registration fees, but the Wings covered their own travel expenses to Bangkok. As the first person of Chinese descent to be elected as a mayor in North America, Peter was looked upon as a celebrity and given special attention throughout the trip. En route the Wings and other mayors from the United States and Canada visited Tokyo, where Mayor Wing made a presentation to the Deputy Mayor on behalf of the City of Kamloops. A similar presentation was made to the Governor of Hong Kong. Because the convention overlapped the Asian Lunar New Year, it provided an enriched cultural experience. The Wings and other delegates took as many side trips as possible, one stop including the bridge made famous by the movie, *The Bridge on the River Kwai*.

On the return trip Peter and Kim travelled to Taiwan, where the red carpet treatment continued. The Taiwanese government provided them with a guide and limousine throughout their stay. They visited the provincial capital, Taichung, where they attended a session of the Legislature. Kim Wing said the list of government officials to be greeted seemed endless.

The highlight of the Taiwan visit was a stop at the Gospel Orphanage where Peter and Kim were "adopted" by the homeless children. Driving into the courtyard they saw a huge banner, "WELCOME THE 1ST MAYOR OF CANADA AND MRS. PETER WIEN" (sic). A large crowd of children sang songs of welcome. After returning to Canada the Wings arranged financial support for ten of the children and paved the way for two to be adopted by a family in Kamloops.

According to Kim, a neighbour asked, "Why did you pick this kid? There were so many of them."

Kim: *"One child looked like the weakest and had to have good care. Canada could do that for him."*

Peter: *"We did arrange for a couple of children to come from the Orient to one of our neighbours here and it turned out very well. [The] boy ended up in electronics [and the] girl studied to be a veterinarian."*

It is clearly evident that service such as this was given out of sincere concern and not for political advantage. The Wings used their position and influence to serve; they did not serve to gain influence and position.

The entire trip, including stops in several countries, numerous meetings and presentations, and side excursions took 28 days in 1967. Their voyage to Hong Kong in 1934 on the liner, Empress of Canada, had taken 21 days each way.

Coincidentally, that same year, 1967, Chinese immigration to Canada was placed on an equal basis with other nationalities. Canada had adhered to the letter of the U.N. Charter of Human rights with the repeal of the Chinese Exclusion Act in 1947, but had applied a different standard in admitting Chinese immigrants as compared to other nationalities. We cannot measure how much the examples and reputations of Chinese Canadians such as Peter and Kim Wing contributed to the change in attitudes of Canadians and elected government officials toward ethnic Chinese.

Early in 1968, W.A.C. Bennett, the Premier of British Columbia, asked Peter to attend the first Constitutional Conference in Ottawa as part of the British Columbia delegation. These meetings were fully televised, a first in Canadian telecommunications. The conference introduced Peter to Pierre Trudeau and Trudeau's vision of Quebec within the greater context of Canada. Peter returned to Kamloops convinced he had met the next Prime Minister of Canada.

The Wings again attended the International Union of Local Authorities convention in 1969. This time the delegates convened in Vienna, Austria. The convention hosted a demonstration of the first computerized city administration and accounting systems. Delegates sat in a movie theatre where cable connection enabled C.W. Mallinson, County Treasurer of West Sussex, Britain to explain and demonstrate the advantages of the computer in city administration. At the time, installation of a computer system was a complex undertaking requiring massive equipment in a large, climate-controlled room. Numerous technicians punched in the programs on dozens, perhaps hundreds, of computer punch cards. The same work can be done today with a good desktop PC. Mallinson assured delegates that the increase in efficiency was well worth the expense. The cost today is minimal by comparison.

During Peter's tenure as Mayor, the City of Kamloops was becoming known both within Canada and abroad not only for its leadership and association with the needs of other municipalities, but also for its cultural contribution to the country. The Kamloops Rube Band was prominent in those years, receiving accolades at the Calgary Stampede, the Pacific National Exhibition in Vancouver and Expo '67 in Montreal. The band was also a smashing success at the New Orleans Mardi Gras and received the gold medal for best foreign band at Expo '70 in Osaka, Japan. The Wings accompanied the band on a European tour. Al Collett of Westwold, BC recalled accompanying Mayor Wing on outings in Europe. He said that band members took on themselves the responsibility to look after Kamloops' beloved mayor.

The Kamloops Native Residential School sponsored a superb Girls' Drum and Bugle Band during Peter's term as Mayor. Bill Mercer, a reporter and city employee, arranged for the band to perform in the Kitchener-Waterloo Octoberfest, the second largest Oktoberfest in the world. Although it literally *"rained on their parade,"* according to Peter, a large crowd turned out and Mayor and Mrs. Wing were there to support the effort. In fact, anything involving Kamloops received the active support and whenever possible, the presence of Mayor Wing.

One of Peter's near accomplishments and great disappointments of that time period was an organisation called "The King's Men." Peter Wing and Ian Clark, an editor involved with Anglican and Roman Catholic publications, started the fraternity in an effort to promote good will, understanding and co-operation between the community churches. The endeavour may have reflected Peter's own experience in the United Church. He had begun Sunday school in the

Methodist Church in 1920. Five years later, St. Andrew's Presbyterian and the Kamloops Congregational churches voted to merge with the Methodist Church. The first combined service was held in June of 1925. The congregations continued with their separate identities until 1927 when they became part of the United Church of Canada. The "King's Men" was intended to extend a similar spirit of mutual respect and harmony between the other churches of Kamloops.

While Bishop Harrington resided over the Catholic Diocese of Kamloops considerable progress was made. Peter and others of the King's Men spoke in the Roman Catholic Church on several occasions. Leading Catholics reciprocated in the United Church, but in 1974, Bishop Exner replaced Harrington in the Kamloops Diocese. With his enforcement of the official stance of the Catholic Church, this early ecumenical movement was discouraged. Without Exner's support the King's Men gradually diminished and finally ceased.

In 1970, Len Marchand, MP for the Kamloops-Cariboo riding and first status Indian to serve as an elected Member of Parliament, raised the possibility of appointing Peter Wing to the Senate or to the Canadian Diplomatic Corps.

In looking back, Peter reflected, *"The thing that I sort of regret was that I might have pushed the appointment to the Senate a little bit more, but because of mother's illness I didn't want to be away from home. Had the people involved been a little more aggressive, I probably would have taken it on. I would have appreciated the Senate."*

In the 1970 Senate appointment Pierre Trudeau opted for Edward M. Lawson, an experienced voice representing labour. Peter expressed regret regarding the lost opportunity. It would have meant continued service to Canada in the political arena, but as the eldest Chinese son, he would not neglect his responsibility to his parents.

"Dad passed in '71, which is the last year I was in City Hall," said Peter. *"We were sort of prepared for it. He had never been ill and just the last couple weeks [before his death] he broke down. I was conducting a council meeting when they phoned. I turned over the meeting and went up [to the hospital]."*

Eng Wing had come to the *Gold Mountain* in 1901 as an illiterate Chinese peasant, lived as a non-person in a British culture for over 45 years and died as a genuine Canadian. Through his children Canada received something far more valuable than gold.

His passing may have been pivotal in Peter's decision to retire. Ancient Chinese tradition placed Lin in the care of her oldest son. Sending her to a senior's residence was out of the question. Kim willingly stepped in to care for her mother-in-law for the next twenty years. She had this to say of Lin's passing, *"She died when she was 99 and her mind was so clear. She thanked me for all the things I had done for her. She said, 'I'm going now. I feel weaker and weaker.' She slowly died and that's it."*

When Peter left City Hall in January of 1972 he could rightly boast that in 12 years he had missed only two city council meetings for personal reasons. What a remarkable record of service and sacrifice on behalf of the community!

Chapter 9

THE PEASANT'S GOLD

Yellow gold...plentiful compared to white-haired friends. (Chinese Proverb)

At a roast in March of 1972, friends hardly generated any heat regarding the Wings. Their course of service had brought them into the presence of a long list of notable public figures. Peter had met people like Robert B. McClure, the respected medical missionary serving in China before World War II. John Diefenbaker and Pierre Trudeau knew him by name. Margaret Trudeau photographed Peter when he received the Order of Canada in 1976. Archbishop Michael Ramsey, Billy Graham and other dignitaries had encountered Mayor Wing of Kamloops. Peter was a personal acquaintance to the three Kamloops Senators – Hewitt Bostock, Syd Smyth and Len Marchand.

Retirement was not a time of idleness. Peter accepted an appointment as Director in the British Columbia Automobile Association, a position he enjoyed for the next 16 years. During his directorship membership in the organisation increased from around 200,000 to over 600,000. As a retiree he also served as a member of the City Court of Revision for Assessments. Having been a realtor, an owner and a member of City Council, Peter appreciated the need for fairness in assessment from all sides.

In the Provincial arena the "retired" Peter Wing was a nominee for Lieutenant Governor of British Columbia in 1978.

"I don't know whether I would want to be Lieutenant Governor," Peter said. *"I've known every Lieutenant Governor in the last fifty years. Some of them were personal friends, so I knew what they were in for."*

The position was given to Henry Bell-Irving who had demonstrated exemplary service in the Second World War. Peter commented regarding the position:

"The average citizen is not aware of the many factors going into such appointments. Such appointments are more than just political reward for years of service well done. Such positions require individuals that can bring their own unique backgrounds, wisdom and public image to the office."

Peter either met or personally knew every Lieutenant Governor of British Columbia who served from 1950 to the year 2000. Regarding such appointments, he added, *"You don't want to live in a goldfish bowl."*

Though family responsibilities limited Peter's travel, retirement opened other doors of service. Peter and Kim represented Kamloops for a visit from Queen Elizabeth and Prince Phillip and later, a visit from Prince Charles and Princess Diana. During the visit by Prince Charles and Princess Diana in 1986, Diana turned to Kim and asked, "How do you manage to keep your heels from sticking in the lawn?" Kim whispered back, *"Flats."* Peter commented regarding the royal family, *"There have been few women like Queen Elizabeth and Princess Diana."*

The Wings continued their support for the United Church of Canada throughout their lives. Peter gave up singing in the choir and rarely attended in his later years, but he and Kim remained paying members of the Kamloops congregation until their move to Vancouver in December of 1998. When the United Church underwent tremendous upheaval over the ordination of gays, the Wings had chosen to remain with the main body. Peter preferred to promote co-operation and reform from within. He found it difficult to accept the stance of Christian fundamentalists.

"The whole society has made too much of it. In Christ's day a hundred people was a crowd; a thousand people was a large city. Today, China, with its population of over one and a quarter billion, has more 'odd' people than the world population of Jesus' day. Jesus said, 'Those of you that are without sin, cast the first stone.'"

The retirement years brought the normal trials of old age. Through it all Peter continued to claim Kim as his best friend, the two were always together and always supportive of each other. In 1986, Kim had major surgery for both hips. After the second operation nurses were at their wits' ends in trying to calm and comfort her during the recovery.

"When I got in the next day, the nurse said, 'We just don't know what to do with her,'" recalled Peter. *"As soon as I touched her, she was fine."*

Peter was admitted to hospital for prostate surgery in 1990. He had not been seriously ill since his back operation in 1954. One of the after-effects of the surgery was an ongoing struggle with occasional vertigo. As the 1990s proceeded, his vision, which had never been strong, began a gradual deterioration. It was not unusual to see the Wings going about their shopping with Kim, ever a servant, driving the car and reading the signs for Peter, much as he had done for his father 75 years earlier. Kim finally turned in the car keys in December of 1998. No more driving. As the year ended, the couple moved to St. Vincent's Langara, an extended care home in Vancouver, British Columbia. There they were closer to Peter's youngest brother, David, and other members of the couple's extended family. Peter continued keeping up with old friends through the Internet and continued following current affairs with the aid of his computer and a large screen television monitor. A young person studying political science would be challenged to stay as informed as Peter Wing on the prevailing state of Canada and the world.

What of Peter's siblings? May, born in 1915, outlived two husbands and eventually settled in Richmond, BC. Lily, born in 1920, made Calgary, Alberta her home. John, born 1924, became the family millionaire. He started as a pharmacist for Shopper's Drug Mart and finished by owning his own pharmaceutical supply house. Jean, born in 1927, retired as a Public Health nurse in 1988 and moved to Nanoose Bay, BC. David, born in 1936, was 22 years younger than Peter. After his retirement from BC Tel he continued to work in the Vancouver real estate market.

Eng Wing continually emphasized education for his children. Only Peter was denied the diplomas and degrees of public education. Kamloops can be thankful for the Chinese tradition that the oldest son be taken into the family business!

Chapter 10

THE FINAL WORD

To talk goodness is not good, only to do goodness is good. (Chinese Proverb)

Peter Wing's greatest fear for Canada was that it become too much like the United States. He considered the amalgamation of large corporations and the influence of the media as threats to the uniqueness of Canadian culture.

"The first thing most people are interested in is the dollar and the second thing is power. Our leaders are not leaders, they're opportunists. Too many lead by rhetoric, not by action. It is more highlighted in our religious community than in other areas. U.S. leaders are just good actors, good speakers. I can't imagine that many of those people think the way they express themselves. If we could only influence our leaders to lead by example."

Regarding the vast differences in foreign policy between Canada and the United States he said, *"It's far better to work with a feather duster than a sledgehammer."*

Kim Wing, who was always involved in a supportive role, succinctly stated the simple philosophy by which Peter served, *"Once you're asked to do something, you do it right to the end."*

A listing of awards and honours gives a summary of the legacy Peter Wing left to his family, friends and community through his faithful service:

Honorary Life Member Kamloops Chamber of Commerce

Life Member Okanagan Mainline Municipal Association

Life Member Union of British Columbia Municipalities

Honorary Life Member British Columbia Automobile Association

Freeman City of Kamloops

Order of Canada, 1976

The foundation stone of the Canadian Honours System established in 1967 by Queen Elizabeth II to recognize outstanding achievement, dedication to the community, and service to the nation.

Queen's Jubilee Medal, 1977

Awarded to individuals deemed to have made significant contributions to fellow citizens, their community, or Canada.

Canadian Council of Christians and Jews Human Relations Award, 1977

Given for outstanding contribution in promoting respect for diversity and understanding between diverse cultures.

Order of British Columbia, 1990

British Columbia's highest form of recognition, established in 1989 to recognize persons who have served with great distinction and excelled in their field in benefiting the people of the Province.

125th Confederation Anniversary Medal, 1992

*Commemorative medal struck by the Royal
Canadian Mint and awarded to Canadians
deemed to have made significant contributions to
their fellow citizens, communities, or Canada.*

Senior Volunteer of the Year for
British Columbia, 1994

Brock House Society recognition for outstanding service.

After so much activity and service, Peter shared some of the frustrations of aging and the gradual decline of health and vitality.

"I had hoped I would be able to do a lot more, but my eyes went and that kind of curtailed [things]. There wasn't much more we would have done… a little more travelling by road. We've been pretty fortunate… had the opportunity of going back to China and [a trip] to Europe.

"I try to keep up on the news. That was one of the reasons I bought the big TV. I used to subscribe to the Vancouver papers, but I depend on what I can hear now."

Peter made an interesting comment about the nature of dreams he was experiencing as his years advanced.

"What I would like to have accomplished and what I wasn't able to do, a fantasy thing. Sometimes it reverts back to the old days when I was responsible for looking after our heating systems and had to crawl through the crawl spaces to repair something. Sometimes my dreams would be along those lines, having to go somewhere to fix something. I don't know what that would mean, but each day I do the best I know how and I'm quite satisfied and happy that I've been in this world this long and I've been able to be part of our society at this time. And if my time comes, well…."

When asked what he would like to be remembered for, Peter said, *"We have a record of what I've done. The last honour as the Senior Volunteer of the Year for British Columbia was about as great an honour as anybody could wish for. If people would follow my example the world would be a better place."*

Asked for an epitaph for his life, he said:

"The record of what a man has done should be sufficient."

Peter Wing suffered a stroke December 15th, 2007 at the age of 93. Kim, who stood by his side through 75 years of marriage, sat by his side at his passing on December 27th, 2007 and joined him in death ten weeks later on March 15th, 2008.

According to Kim, following the Chinese tradition that the oldest member of the family keep a piece of gold, some gold coins had been passed to Peter by his father. She gave the last coin to one of her nephews. Eng Wing, a young peasant from China, came to the *Gold Mountain* of Canada to seek his fortune in 1901. Through his oldest son, Peter Wing, he left a legacy far more valuable than a piece of gold.

Peter and Kim Wing, side by side for seventy-five years, 1932 - 2007
(Photos courtesy of Peter & Kim Wing)

Epilogue

In the spring of 1996 my wife, Linda, and I received our Canadian citizenship after having lived as immigrants in Canada for almost 25 years. That year the Canadian government appointed leading citizens to preside as citizenship judges across the country. What a treat to see Peter Wing escorted to the stage by an RCMP officer in full dress uniform. What an honour to stand before this wonderful man and take the oath of allegiance to the Queen.

After the ceremony, Linda and I lingered outside the Kamloops Legion Hall. The proceedings were finished and the attendees were gone. Coming out the door, a cane in one hand and a box of dishes in the other, was Peter Wing. Behind him walked Kim, carrying coffee supplies that had been served to the group. Peter had presided over the proceedings. Kim, a member of the Soroptimist Club International, had served the refreshments. They had contributed their own dishes for use by the new Canadians and had stayed after to help clear the hall. It struck me that even with all their accomplishments and prestige, Peter and Kim continued to serve in heart and in deed. To us they will always be the Honorable Peter and Kim Wing!

Acknowledgements

In the fall of 1995 while taking an extension course in writing, I wrote a feature article about Joanna Walters who was at the time directing a literacy program for street people. Joanna was thrilled with the support for her program and suggested Peter Wing as a worthy subject, going so far as to give me Mr. Wing's phone number. I owe her thanks for putting me in contact with such a remarkable person.

The first manuscript was considered too short for publication by regional publishers who suggested it might be appropriate as part of an anthology of Canadian Chinese history. At that point the project was placed "on the shelf." I offered to print and bind a limited edition, but Peter Wing wanted something more, so the project sat. I'm certain that Peter was beginning to wonder if it would be completed while he still lived (he was in his 80s). Peter introduced me to Robert Goss, a local publisher he had seen interviewed on television. Robert saw the value of the material and encouraged me to rewrite that first manuscript. We then published *The Peasant's Gold*, a small, succinct edition of Peter Wing's life story.

Now over twenty years later, I have taken the time to improve and expand the material. I must thank my editor, Erin McMullan, for her countless hours of work on the manuscript and her direction in bringing to life much of the historical content. Erin's input has been invaluable.

The greatest thanks must be to Peter and Kim Wing themselves who gave me countless hours of their time and access to their personal photos, newspaper clippings and awards. Both have been deceased for some time now. Though Peter was grateful for the original book, I feel he would be very pleased with this edition which places his story in the context of the larger Canadian Chinese community and its struggle for its rightful place in Canadian society.

About the Author

Terrence Roth and his wife Linda immigrated to Canada from the United States in 1972. In the course of his work as a church pastor, Terrence has lived in British Columbia, Saskatchewan, Ontario and Newfoundland. He and his wife received their Canadian citizenship in 1996.

The Peasant's Gold was first published in 1999. This revised version had to wait for Roth's retirement and includes additional research and quotations from the original interviews with Peter Wing and his wife, Kim. Roth has also written features for church publications and local newspapers. His article, "The Saint of Labrador," a biographical sketch of the medical missionary, Sir Wilfred Grenfell, received first place honours for non-fiction writing in the 1995 God Uses Ink Christian Writing Awards presented by Faith Today and the Mennonite Reporter.

Roth currently lives in Kamloops, British Columbia where he pursues his writing, involvement in community theatre and support of local churches through pulpit supply and occasional interim pastoring.

Bibliography

Balf, Mary. *Kamloops: A History of the District up to 1914*. Kamloops: Kamloops Museum Association, 1981.

Balf, Ruth. *Kamloops 1914-1945*. Kamloops: Kamloops Museum Association, 1975.

bc.united-church.ca/archives, *S.S. Osterhout*, 1-24-16.

Berton, Pierre. *The Last Spike*. McClelland and Stewart Limited, 1974.

Canadian Encyclopedia, *Radio and Television Broadcasting*, 1-26-16.

canadianorangehistoricalsite.com/SSOsterhout.php, 1-30-16.

chinaculturecorner.com, 1-27-16.

Chinese Proverbs from Olden Times. Mount Vernon, Peter Pauper Press, 1956.

Chong, Denice. *The Concubine's Children*. Toronto: Penguin, 1995.

Choy, Jason. *The Jade Peony*. Douglas & McIntyre, 1995.

Encyclopedia of British Columbia, *Klu Klux Klan.*

familylovetoknow.com/chinese-family-values, 1-31-16.

Marchand, Len and Hughes, Matt. *Breaking Trail.*
Prince George: Caitlin Press Inc., 2000.

Morton, James. *In the Sea of Sterile Mountains: The Chinese in British Columbia.* J.J. Douglas Ltd., 1974.

Morse, J.J., *Kamloops: The Inland Capital, A Condensed History,* 1957.

pages.ucsd.edu/~dkjordan/chin/familism.html, 1-26-16.

pne.ca, *100 Years of Fun,* 1-25-16.

Thompson Rivers History and Heritage Society, *Kamloops: Trading Post to Tournament Capital,* 2012.

travelchinaguide.com, *Happy 2016 Chinese New Year,* 1-27-16.

Ward, Peter J., *The Oriental Immigrant and Canada's Protestant Clergy 1858-1925,* ojs.library.ubc.ca, 1-23-16.

xroads.virginia.edu, *Radio in the 1920s,* 1-27-16.

CPSIA information can be obtained
at www.ICGtesting.com
Printed in the USA
LVOW11s0520100917

548139LV00001B/14/P